NEVER SAY NO

MY JOURNEY FROM SADDLEWORTH TO SAIGON

A MEMOIR

KENNETH ATKINSON OBE

EARNSHAW BOOKS

Never Say No

By Kenneth Atkinson OBE

Trade Paper: 978-988-8904-41-9
Digital: 978-988-8904-40-0

BIOGRAPHY & AUTOBIOGRAPHY

EB241

Published in Hong Kong by Earnshaw Books Ltd.

Contents

1

THE ICE CREAM PRINCE OF SHEFFIELD

On a cold evening in September of 1966, I arrived in the old steel town of Sheffield, by train via Rotherham, with a feeling of trepidation, my university life ahead of me. I entered my hall of residence, an old stone building that was to be my home for the next one, two, or three years, and did not really feel much better. The next day, my very first day as a university student, I walked down to the university campus to register for my classes. I passed terraced stone houses, a couple of pubs, and some chip shops, and I met a few other new students including Mike Pratt, who was also registering for his first year and for the same course as myself. He is still a friend to this day. Mike became not just one of my first university friends, but also my first business partner. He asked me to join his ice cream business, which he had started to earn extra money. I had previously worked part time in a bakery for a while, and did the usual post office gig during Christmas, but this sounded like a much better option.

Of course, Sheffield University was a far cry from my previous education experience, the William Morris County Technical school, where class attendance had been compulsory. Suddenly, I had the freedom of choice to attend lectures, or to simply not go at all. I chose to attend most of them, but I still had quite a bit of free time to study and play!

Sheffield then was more of a village than a town, even though it was a cathedral city. It was rather dull, but it provided easy access to the Pennines and the Peak District and was not too far from Manchester where I went to watch my beloved Manchester United as often as I could, hitchhiking over the Snake Pass to get to Old Trafford.

The ice cream business was one of my very first truly entrepreneurial ventures. It was also an early lesson in how retail businesses actually work, and it all began on the streets and small cul-de-sacs of Sheffield.

Mike had two vans and allocated to me the older van, a 1948 Morris J, a former post office van with windows and new lettering on its side panels proudly marketing 'Mike's Ices'. There was no refrigeration, just insulated cabinets with inserts frozen overnight in brine tanks. As a first-year student at the University of Sheffield, I was keen to earn some extra cash during the mid-term breaks and weekends by scooping out ice cream for kids. Simple enough gig, no? All kids like ice cream, so what could go wrong? Well, it turned out to be not so simple.

When I met him, Mike was looking for a partner and I immediately jumped into the venture, handling the sales and marketing part. Driving a van around town, turning on the musical chimes of 'Popeye The Sailor Man' to advertise my arrival at various stops on my chosen route, seemed like a pretty easy job. Once I stopped and started the music, the little kids would line up beside the van, and I would serve them ice cream. It all made sense in theory and initially it worked in practice too. The 'Popeye The Sailor Man' chime did the trick. It pulled the kids in and we had a small gathering of kids right from the start at each chosen stop.

What a great way to earn a bit of money! Drive around, play a little song, scoop out ice cream for kids and get paid for it while *also* making kids happy. Perfect. We had a good range of products as well. I doled out cones of vanilla ice cream, some with raspberry vinegar, some with flakes, and some with bubble gum. We had plain ice creams and chocolate wafers, and also tubs. I had to work fast in order to keep up with demand, but that was a good problem to have because I was making money

with every scoop. For a first-year student about to enter the second year, it was a welcome, and paying, business internship.

But our competition saw it all a bit differently. This was the Italian ice cream vendors, Sanella's. I had no idea there was a mini-mafia within the ice cream business, but there most definitely was in Sheffield in those years. I also hadn't known that there were so many big, burly, strong Italian men who were making a living by selling ice cream. But there were, and they did not appreciate a naïve university student horning in on their living.

One day, having figured out how to pitch ice cream and the best streets on which to do it, I was parked in a cul-de-sac and saw a Sanella's ice cream van speeding towards me. I immediately guessed that something was wrong. It squealed to a stop in front of my van, blocking off any chance for an escape, and two big men jumped out. One confronted me directly while the other snatched the keys out of the ignition of my van. These blokes were serious.

"You think you can come onto our turf, boy?" said the one who confronted me directly. "Let's see how well you can sell melted ice cream."

They blocked me there for a couple of hours and poured all my raspberry vinegar into the tub of vanilla ice cream. Then they drove away taking the keys to my van with them, and I could only sit and watch as my inventory slowly turned to soup in the summer heat. Eventually, they returned and threw the keys on the ground.

Business Lesson Number One: Know your competition.

Business Lesson Number Two: Think fast and adapt to market conditions, especially when the competition consists of big, angry Italian types who steal your keys and ruin your inventory.

Sitting in that cup-de-sac after the Italians had left, I had to think fast and adapt faster than the amount of time it takes for ice cream to melt and have zero value to the neighbourhood kids who loved it cold and creamy. The Mike's Ices van continued to broadcast the catchy Popeye song to all within earshot, and the neighbourhood kids continued to crowd around the van pleading for ice cream. I thought fast and I adapted faster. Bowls instead of cones and an on-the-spot two for one deal on price.

"Hey kids!" I declared with a big smile. "We have a technical problem here, but we still have plenty of raspberry ripple that is now available in bowls instead of cones. We also have a special deal for all of you. Two scoops for the price of one! And I only have raspberry ripple left! What do you say?"

To my amazement, they loved it. As it turned out, the Sheffield locals were more than happy to eat ice cream from a bowl as opposed to from a cone. For those who lived in the grim housing estates of post-war England, ice cream was ice cream and a two-for-one deal was too good to pass up. By the end of the day, I had sold most of my melted inventory and turned what had threatened to be a financial disaster into a moderate success.

I survived my first small battle with the Italians, but the ice cream wars continued. Business Lessons Three, Four, Five and Six, and beyond were quickly learned and absorbed. For example, I learned the importance of timing and would arrive at the most popular spots just before my Italian competitors. It became a game of cat and mouse and I got pretty good at it.

There were, however, several close calls and narrow escapes. One time I was cornered near my university with a group of angry Italians advancing on me with tire irons. My survival instincts kicked in and I abandoned the van (as well as Business Lessons One to at least Ten) and sprinted across the campus, with the sound of clanging metal echoing behind me. Another time, I spent a terrifying afternoon hiding under a bed at the ice cream supplier's warehouse while the Italians roamed around trying to find me, shouting threats at the supplier in broken English. It was a far cry from the idyllic summer job I had envisioned at the beginning of the summer, but I actually thrived on the adrenaline and the challenge.

Mike's Ices had some perks as well. It funded my budding romance with a pretty nurse from Sheffield Royal Infirmary, much to the chagrin of my parents who noticed that I was not at home, in London, very often. More importantly, I was learning valuable lessons about business, including how to deal with competition, and how to create new strategies on the fly. These were skills that would serve me well in the years to come.

Over the summer and into my third and final year of university, I not only survived but thrived in Sheffield's cutthroat ice cream scene. I developed a loyal customer base, perfected my scooping technique, and even managed to forge an uneasy truce with some of the Italian vendors. But I knew that the real world awaited beyond the cozy confines of Sheffield and university life, and I was eager to expand my horizons.

And expand them I did. I am a little bit far from home for someone born and raised in Great Britain. Nearly seventy-seven years later, I have ended up in my new home in the city of Saigon (Ho Chi Minh City), Vietnam. It's been my "new home" for the past 34 years. Life can be quite a grand journey, and mine at least certainly has been.

When I embarked on my business career over fifty years ago, the landscape was vastly different from today. Back then, formality reigned supreme. Instead of modern accounting software, we relied on IBM accounting machines. The internet was non-existent, and printed newspapers and magazines were our primary sources of information. Emails, fax machines and cell phones were things of the future, and we conducted business using regular phones and telex machines.

Throughout my extensive career, I've witnessed a remarkable evolution in business tools and technologies. Adapting to these changes has been crucial for survival and success. While I've faced my share of failures, my ability to embrace these new tools, as well as different cultures, has ultimately led to my achievements. Now, as an Independent Director of a number of companies, I'm navigating the complexities of AI, both from a personal perspective and that of an Independent Director's responsibilities.

However, one business tool that has remained constant throughout my career is networking, which I now largely conduct in my private bar, The Nag's Head, located in my home in the Binh Thanh District of Ho Chi Minh City (Saigon). The Nag's Head features a marble countertop, high stools, a stunning view of Saigon, along with a blend of modern and traditional art. It also boasts a vast collection of spirits, wines, beers, and soft drinks. But the true essence of The Nag's Head lies in the networking that happens within it.

I've been both a bartender and customer, starting during my university days at Sheffield University during the 1960s. While studying economics, accounting, and law, I also learned invaluable lessons from behind the bar. From the first drinks poured, I recognised the importance of networking, meeting new people, and sharing ideas. The bar was a hub for exchanging information and

building relationships, a practice that remains just as relevant today as it was then.

But to go back to the beginning, or the first eight years of my life, my parents and my little brother and I lived amid the stone walls and pastoral fields of Saddleworth, on the edge of the moors in the north of England. There were relatively few people in the area and, in post-war England, even fewer employment opportunities for people like my father. Life was a struggle. Our nearest "big city" was the industrial centre of Manchester, which at its peak in the 1950s might have had a population of two million people. Back then, Saddleworth's only claim to fame was a plane crash on the moors, in 1949, that killed 24 passengers and crew. Later on, it was also the burial site for two serial killers, Myra Hindley and Ian Brady, who buried their victims on the moors in the mid-1960s and thus earned the moniker, "The Moors Murderers."

My career of global business travel and knowing first-hand how difficult (and rewarding) international travel can be, makes me appreciate just how impressive my Mum's journey was.

Mum circa 1946 in the Hotel Garden in Cairo

It's not a stretch to say that she was born with a silver spoon in her mouth. She was born and raised in a high-end hotel in the Egyptian capital, Cairo, and for certain was pampered by the hotel staff, because her parents, my grandparents, owned the hotel. They had the money and connections to send their daughter and her four siblings to the best local French schools and hired governesses to take care of her while they were busy running the hotel. Imagine growing up in the 1930s and 1940s in such a palace of a hotel, surrounded by staff who catered to your every need!

My maternal Grandparents Daniel and Henriette

My Dad was a plain-clothes secret intelligence officer in the Royal Air Force (RAF), and my Mum met him when she was just fourteen or maybe even younger. One day, after taking her to school in his jeep, when he knew the war was coming to an end and that he was going to have to return to England, he asked her parents if they could marry. He was ten years older than my Mum, and her parents refused, but offered her elder sister in my Mum's place. My Dad turned her down, and in the end my grandparents agreed that if my Mum still wanted to marry him when she was sixteen years old, they would allow her to go to England. Inevitably, love prevailed and on or about her sixteenth birthday, she set sail for England. When my Mum was seventeen and my Dad was twenty-seven, they got married, and they settled in Austerlands, on the outskirts of Oldham and the edge of the Saddleworth moors.

For my Mum, England was an entirely new world. She had to transition from life in a 5-star hotel in Cairo with servants and

Mum setting sail for England aged sixteen

governesses who did everything for you, to post-World War II Britain, where she had to do everything herself. The norm was living on war rations in coal-fired heated homes. My Mum had never boiled an egg or even made a cup of tea, then suddenly, here she was, expected to light fires and cook meals with rationed food. But she was resourceful, and I remember her being able to get extra meat rations from our local butcher. Incredible! An interesting true story was that my Mum's younger sister came over from Egypt for the wedding and actually fell in love with the son of our neighbours in Heywood Avenue, and they also married.

It was even harder for my Dad. It's fair to say that he was a victim of the post-war economy. When he wasn't completely unemployed, he regularly had to juggle a number of different jobs in the early years after the war. Amongst other jobs, he worked for a time as a lorry driver and a salesman for a white goods company, basically doing whatever he could to keep food on the table and a roof over our heads. We did own an end-of-terrace house, but it was stressful and I sometimes bore the brunt of this stress. He was a strict man and not afraid to use his hand or his razor sharpening belt.

Mum and Dad's wedding day in 1947 with her sister and brother-in-law

In 1953, my Mum became

seriously ill with Miliary Tuberculosis, which would have killed her had it not been for a new drug (Streptomycin), which they trialed on my Mum. In fact at one point, I was told that my mother had gone to live with Jesus. During this period, I was shipped from pillar-to-post, and was often left anxiously waiting for my Dad to come home, seemingly having forgotten that he had told me to go to stay with one auntie or another. My little brother Philip and I were shuttled back and forth between aunts and uncles, but it was my paternal grandparents who really stepped up.

Mum back in Cairo 1954 with my brother Phillip and great grandfather

It was a very lonely and sometimes worrying time for me. After my Mum was discharged from hospital, she went on

With my brother in Carnforth at my paternal grandparents' home in 1954

convalescence to Egypt for a few months. I missed my mother and my younger brother and did not have any real friends of my age around me. Back then, my grandfather was a station foreman (later to become a station master) at Carnforth Station, near Lancaster, through which the London-to-Scotland railway line passed and where the Barrow-in-Furnace line started.

My grandfather introduced me to the world of trains and I'm still fascinated with them and with rail travel in general because of him. For a little kid, in that portion of my life at least, I was living a dream. Because of my grandfather, I was often able to cab the engines that stopped in Carnforth, en route to Scotland, and travel in the cab of the shunting engines as the carriages were shunted around the yard. I still remember that time clearly. In some ways, it was magical, but in others it was very lonely. Whilst my grandparents were very kind and caring, they had not been brought up in an era of showing love and affection. This also involved another change of school. I attended the infant's school in Warton, a school my father had attended in his younger years.

At Heywood Avenue with my Mum, brother, Nana, and cousin Diane in 1956

When I was around nine years old, my Dad got a new job in London. So we all said goodbye to our home at 9 Heywood Avenue, on the edge of Saddleworth moors with its fields surrounded by stone walls and moved to the big city of London. My Dad's job was not exactly what he had expected, but our life became a bit better in terms of living conditions. It was an expensive place to live in, though, so my Mum had to work in order to keep things "above the line", as we used to say. Life was more comfortable. After my Dad changed jobs in 1958 and before I moved into my teenage years, it was all good. My Mum, however, had to adjust again. First it had been the shift from life in a luxury hotel to the alien environment of northwest England, Now, it was from countryside living to big city living. But she, and therefore we, managed.

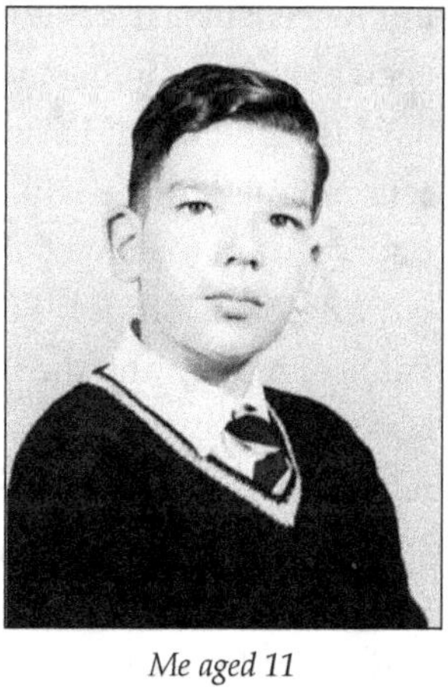

Me aged 11

My parents had exceptional work ethics, and they were financially resourceful as well. My Mum was the frugal one and not at all careless with money. That didn't mean we also didn't have fun even if things were a bit tight. I remember our family going to the Plessey Social Club in Ilford on Saturday evenings. My dad, my brother, and I would play snooker, and then we would have fish and chips, from a local chippie, before heading home. As any British person of that era will tell you, it was tough after the end of the war. Obviously, the country had to rebuild its businesses, infrastructure, economy, and so on. Everyone had to dig deep into whatever they had inside of them to get by and get over those challenges.

There is one childhood memory that I will never forget. One winter's day, I was sent to our local shop in Austerlands with a single shilling, the last shilling that my family had at the time, to buy a loaf of bread. I was told to buy the bread and that the change from the bread was just enough to cover the bus fare for my dad to collect his dole money the next day. Off I went, trudging through the snow, clutching carefully in my gloved hands the very last shilling my family possessed. Somehow, I dropped the shilling in the snow. Imagine my horror and fear when I returned home without bread or money. My father dragged me through the snow, retracing my steps and trying to find the shilling, but to no avail.

Looking back though, I can say with confidence that the careful money management that I witnessed by my mother, along with the exceptionally strong work ethic of my father, heavily influenced me. It gave me a solid foundation to do what I've been able to do in business over the many years since. Working hard is a given, but I also learned to have, I think, good financial sense. I guess that's what happens when you grow up relatively poor, with parents who always stepped up to their financial and work responsibilities. From a very early age, I appreciated the value of money and the importance of living within one's means. My parents liked to entertain and that is one of my passions, which I also owe to my parents.

My school years were uneventful except for the number of schools I attended (seven in total) and that I was an 11+ failure and had two years in a secondary modern school in Ilford, before passing my 13+ exam and moving to the William Morris County Technical School in Walthamstow London E1. My new school resulted in quite a daily journey. I had to walk for 15 minutes then take a 20 to 30-minute bus ride from Gants Hill to Gainsford Road. But I enjoyed the school and we had a class of 13+ entrants and bonded together well. The headmaster and headmistress were very strict even down to sock inspections after assembly. On one occasion, I was wearing black socks instead of grey and was sent home to change them. I managed to earn reasonable grades for my O and A levels and got into my second-choice university—Sheffield University to study for a BA Honours in economics, accountancy, and law.

Many years ago, and actually not long after I had started traveling abroad after university, I was unexpectedly reminded of my parents and the upbringing they gave to my brother and I. It was in 1978 and I was on a plane flying back to England from my first overseas months-long posting in Singapore. I started chatting to my seat mate (there I go, networking again) and we quickly learned that we were both from Austerlands. The guy started talking about a newspaper shop that he owned which, as it turned out, was right across the street from my childhood home.

I told the guy this and he looked at me with total disbelief and said, "Bloody hell, your father is Albert Atkinson? He was my really good friend."

When I related this story to my Dad, he was equally incredulous. He said that this guy had emigrated to Australia more than twenty years prior and had never returned. He was actually returning then because his sister had passed away. That might have been my very first "It's a small world after all" moment. I've had many since then, but that one was inspirational and made me even more excited about international travel and

Albert Turners newspaper shop in Austerlands

business. It seems that no matter how far you travel, you can never truly escape your roots. My roots were in Austerlands in Saddleworth, and I have never forgotten that fact.

2

European Adventures

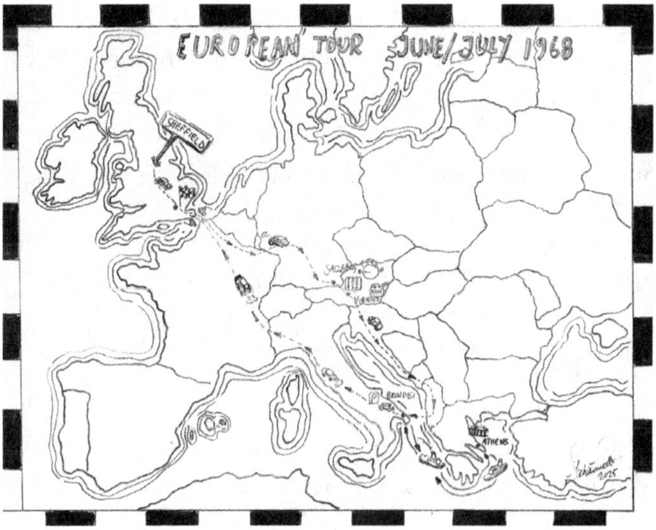

And so it was that with a spirit of adventure and self confidence, I along with my friends Mike and Keith, hatched a plan for an epic European tour during our summer break in 1968. We initially set our sights on America, but Europe, with its rich history and diverse cultures, also beckoned and won out.

We faced our first challenge before we even left British soil. Back then, there were strict foreign exchange controls, which meant we could only take £30 each out of the country, with an extra £15 for petrol coupons. This necessitated careful planning and creative packing. Half of the backseat of Keith's Morris 1100 car was filled with boxes of food. These would be our staple provisions for the journey across the European continent.

As we boarded the ferry to cross the Channel, I couldn't help but feel a mixture of excitement and trepidation. The open road lay ahead, promising adventure and the unknown. Little did I know just how eventful the trip would prove to be, and how significantly it would impact on my life.

Our first stop was Brussels, where our lack of camping experience became painfully apparent. In our haste to pack, we forgot tent pegs and a groundsheet. So as rain poured down on our first night of camping, turning our campsite into a muddy quagmire, we huddled miserably under a leaking tent wondering if we had bitten off more than we could chew.

After seeing the main sites of Brussels and eating the famous frites, we pressed on. Our limited budget, along with the foreign currency exchange controls, meant that we sometimes had to pass by major tourism sites. We also camped every night because we could not afford hotels. We drove on through Luxembourg, past the catacombs, and into Germany where we immediately made a stop in Saarburg for German sausages and sauerkraut before heading on into Austria with a stop in Munich, sadly before Ocktoberfest.

When we arrived in the picturesque city of Salzburg, and after finding a campsite and pitching our tent, with newly bought groundsheet and tent pegs, our journey took its first dramatic turn. After a night of revelry in a beer garden, just below the castle grounds, drinking large beers (actually one litre steins), I gallantly (if somewhat foolishly) attempted to escort an inebriated English girl back to the campsite, where we had pitched our tent and where she and her boyfriend had pitched theirs. He, however, had departed the scene early, as he was not happy with the amount of beer his girlfriend was consuming. Unfortunately, my chivalrous act was misinterpreted by local police, which resulted in the one and only time I have ever spent time in a jail cell, with me trying to explain my actions to the Salzburg police in broken German.

"Ich bin ein schuler," I repeated over and over to their deaf ears. [I am a student.]

I was hoping that my terrible German would convince the police officers of my naiveté and innocence. But either they didn't care or really didn't understand what I was trying to say in my lousy German. Eventually, they let me go with a stern warning, and I made a couple of mental notes, firstly to brush up on my German, and secondly to be more cautious in future in my attempts at gallantry. Thankfully, I found my way back to the campsite and was glad to be reunited with Mike and Keith.

The misadventures continued as we made our way to the city of Vienna. In one mishap, we ran out of petrol on the autobahn. This led to me hitching a ride with a bewildered Austrian family to find fuel for our car. I eventually found some at the end of the motorway about 20 miles away and just outside Vienna. Unfortunately, the motorway was still under construction and was closed in the opposite direction. I had no Google maps, no mobile phone, and only a can of petrol in my possession, and I had to find a way back to our car by hitching two rides. Eventually, as I got close to where Mike and Keith had been waiting, I watched as my friends were being towed, away by friendly policemen in the direction of a patrol station while I was trying to explain to my hitchhike hosts, a family of non-English speakers, what was happening. It was a comedy of errors that tested our resourcefulness and friendship, but in the end we managed to reunite and continue our journey. After a couple of nights in Vienna, we decided to drive up to Kahlenberg, a village outside

Vienna. As we passed through, we heard music and then saw a procession of people in the street all singing and dancing, so we stopped and parked the car so we could investigate what was going on. We soon learnt that the first grapes had been picked, and we joined the villagers in celebrating with lots of wine and great hospitality. They welcomed us and plied us with food and wine as the procession visited all the local bars and restaurants in the village. The next day, with lingering hangovers, we drove off in the direction of Yugoslavia. We passed through Gras, crossed the border at Spiel Feld and then drove on to our first stop in Ljubljana.

At that time, Yugoslavia was a federation of six republics—Slovenia, Croatia, Bosnia and Herzegovina, Montenegro, Macedonia, and Serbia. As we drove south, the landscape changed dramatically. The rolling hills gave way to rugged coastlines, and the air became heavy with the scent of the Adriatic. We drove down the coast looking for a stop that would offer work, so we could replenish our rapidly dwindling cash reserves. We continued down the coast, stopping in Rijeka and Split before reaching Dubrovnik, and got as far as the Albanian border, a frontier of the unknown in those Cold War days. Dubrovnik was an amazing experience and the first walled city I had visited. We stopped there for a few days to look for work, without success. The food did not leave a lasting impression, but the Slivovitz, a vicious Yugoslavian plum brandy, certainly did.

It was at a petrol station near the Albanian border that I experienced another one of those uncanny coincidences that make travel so magical. A voice called out, "Hey, didn't you used to go to William Morris County Technical School?"

I turned around to find myself face to face with a former schoolmate, now on his own European adventure. The world, it seemed, was smaller than I had ever imagined.

From Bari in Yugoslavia, we decided to cut short the driving and the petrol consumption, so we took a car ferry to Brindisi in Italy, and parked our trusty Morris 1100 in a parking area near the port, as we embarked on another sea voyage to Athens. The journey took us through the Corinth Canal, an artificial waterway which connects the Gulf of Corinth and the Aegean and reduces the length of the journey by 700 km. We were awestruck by the sheer walls of the narrow passage towering above us as our ferry squeezed through.

Athens was also a revelation. The Parthenon, perched atop the Acropolis, stood as a testament to ancient glory. I found myself transported back in time as I wandered through the ruins, imagining the city as it must have been at the height of its power. But even here, in the cradle of Western civilisation, my penchant for misadventure followed me. One sweltering night, for example, I returned to our hotel room to find it filled with mosquitoes, drawn by the lights we had carelessly left on and the windows that we had left open. We did enjoy the Greek food, but not the Retsina wine, which I have never taken to. The Ouzo, an aniseed-based drink similar to Pastis, was a great alternative.

The Acropolis in Athens

We made our way back to Italy to retrieve our car and headed for Naples where our luck took a turn for the worse. We decided to have a blow out with our remaining limited funds, but while we were having a memorable Italian meal in a family restaurant, our car was broken into and my camera and all my precious films were stolen. The photographic record of our grand adventure was gone, leaving us with only memories and a harsh lesson about the realities of travel.

By the time we pointed our dirty Morris 1100 northward, bound for home, we were running on pretty much nothing but fumes – both literally and figuratively. Our money was almost gone, the food supplies exhausted and our energy depleted. But as we crossed back into France and caught sight of the English Channel, I realised that we had gained something far more valuable than photographs or souvenirs. We had gained experience, a modicum of resilience, and a broader perspective on the world.

Returning to Sheffield for my third and final year at university, I found himself changed by my summer adventures. The ice cream wars and European escapades had instilled in me a confidence and street-smartness that set me apart from many of my peers.

With this new attitude, I threw himself into university life with renewed vigour. As the re-elected entertainment secretary for my hall of residence, I was at the centre of Sheffield's vibrant music scene. Through a connection with a booking agency called Penny Lane, I began arranging gigs separate from the main university events, which became the stuff of university legend.

The University Campus Entertainment booked groups including The Who, Janis Joplin, Julie Driscoll, the Brian Auger Trinity, and the Bonzo Dog Doo-Dah Band, while I organised smaller gigs at the Hall of Residence. With the help of the agents from Penny Lane, I developed a knack for spotting up-and-coming talent, booking bands just before they hit the big time. This "knack" sometimes meant having to renegotiate contracts when a group which suddenly found themselves in the Top 10. One of these was Joe Cocker and his band, and while he honoured the contract, he played for a much shorter period than the agreed time. Another was the Vantennas, a well-known backing group which was supporting the Rolling Stones at a gig around the time we hired them.

My university years weren't all rock 'n roll and adventures, however. The looming spectre of exams cast a shadow over my final year. Unlike the practical challenges I had faced selling ice cream or navigating foreign lands, these academic hurdles were my Achilles' Heel. Simply put, exams and I didn't like each other much. The pressure of having my entire academic career judged on the basis of a few hours in an examination hall weighed heavily on me. There were sleepless nights, frantic revision sessions, and moments of doubt when I wondered if I would make it through.

But in the end, I emerged with an honours degree in Finance and Accounting. It was a pass that did not set the academic world alight, but it represented a hard-won personal triumph. As I stood in my graduation gown, diploma in hand, I reflected on the journey that had brought me to this point.

Graduation 1969

It's been decades now, but I still look back on my university days with a mix of nostalgia and amusement. The Honours degree that had seemed so important at the time became little more than a footnote in my life. In fact, it was the lessons learned outside the classroom—in the streets of Sheffield, on the roads of Europe, and in the bustling student union—that truly defined my university experience, as well as had the most impact on my career. The ice cream wars taught me about competition, quick thinking, and the importance of understanding your market. The European adventure broadened my horizons and tested my resilience and adaptability. And my role as entertainment secretary honed my organisational skills and eye for talent.

More than any textbook or lecture, it was these experiences which shaped me into the person I was destined to become. As I prepared to step out into the world beyond university, I carried with me not just a degree, but a wealth of real-world experience that would prove invaluable in the years to come. I could lay claim, with only a slight stretch of the imagination, to being the "Ice Cream Prince of Sheffield" who later became a successful businessman because I constantly drew upon the skills I had honed during those formative years. I may not have become a rock star or a world-renowned academic, but I discovered something far more valuable, the ability to adapt, persevere, and find opportunity in the most unlikely of places.

I tell my children and grandchildren some of the stories of my youthful adventures, and we laugh. I've always encouraged my kids and grandkids to respect formal education, but also never to underestimate the education you get outside the classroom. University teaches you many things, but life teaches you even more. There is enduring value in experience, resilience, and a willingness to embrace the unexpected twists and turns of life's great journey. This mostly happens when you step outside of a classroom and leave your comfort zone.

When I got to Sheffield, I initially enrolled for a BA Honours Degree in Economics, Accountancy, and Law with the intention of joining the accountancy profession, which would have exempted me up to the intermediate stage of the ACCA accountancy exams. But at the last minute, I decided that the accountancy profession was not for me (ironic, as I ended up there anyway), and before graduation I applied to several merchant banks to join their graduate training programs. This is when I learned a little about the City of London and the importance of where one is formally educated, as well as a person's family background. When first interviewing at a new bank, the common question asked was what school did you go to and what did your father do for a living. It soon became obvious that it was going to be difficult for me to penetrate this divide. But I persevered and travelled to London for several interviews until one day something clicked at my interview with the HR Director of Kleinwort Benson. I was offered my first real job with a salary of 100 pounds per month.

That was in 1969. It was where my legacy started.

3

Global Banker

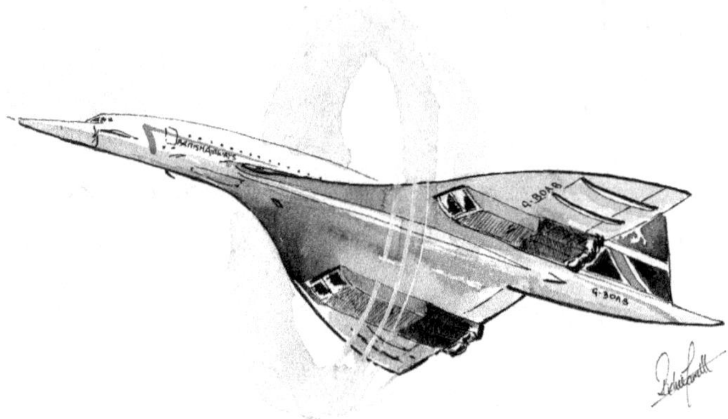

My first real job was with Kleinwort Benson, a London merchant bank, as a graduate trainee, and it was the one that gave me an initial taste of what an international banking career could be like. At Kleinwort Benson, I spent time in most of the departments as part of my induction program, but my favourite was the trading room. I expressed a desire to try a career in trading, but I was told by the head of trading activities at the bank, "You are too qualified and too old to be a trader. We need younger people who have an instinct for trading."

I then joined the Export Finance Department where I got exposure to international loans guaranteed by the UK government's Export Credit Guarantee Department. Our role was to assist UK exporters win contracts by being able to offer a form of subsidised financing, and the amounts were not small. I worked on a large deal for the Algerian State-Owned Oil Company, Sonatrac, and an even bigger one for the Come by Chance Oil refinery in Newfoundland. At the time I was living with my parents in Chigwell in Essex, commuting to work on the London Underground. I also got a good taste of how bankers, in those years at least, entertained themselves and their clients. There was a whole floor in the offices at 20 Fenchurch Street devoted to dining rooms for the directors. The regular routine was gin and tonics, white wine with the starter, red wine with the main course, and then port with the cheese. The port was served in a traditional decanter that could not rest on the table because of its shape. This meant it just kept going around the table until it was empty. How people managed to still work after those indulgent lunches was something that I never really figured out.

So much for my career in trading and export finance. I left Kleinwort Benson in 1971 after just 18 months, and was offered a more interesting and better paying job with a consortium bank, Western American Bank Europe Limited, as an assistant manager on double my previous salary. The bank was owned by Midland Bank, Wells Fargo, National Bank of Detroit and Security Pacific and it was located in Finsbury Circus in a grand old building, just round the corner from Liverpool Station. I learned a lot there about credit appraisals and syndicated loans. This was mainly from my American bosses who had been trained at Citibank. It was a sumptuous environment. The offices were lavish and the directors' dining room was something to behold, as was the food and alcohol consumption. I worked on a couple of interesting transactions including one for Telefonos de Mexico and one for the Venezuelan National Oil Company. Our role was to negotiate market terms with the borrower, then syndicate the loan while negotiating the loan documentation. However, I was still keen to progress my career.

In 1971, I also got married at the age of 23 to that pretty nurse I mentioned earlier. We bought a detached bungalow in Colchester in Essex, as housing in London, even with access to a cheap mortgage, was too expensive for first-time buyers. Colchester was a medieval town with a castle and good train connections to Liverpool Street Station in London, with fast trains making the journey in just one hour. My first son Jim was born while I was still at the bank in 1973.

Not too long after that, in early 1974 and not long before my daughter Claire was born, I was recruited to work at Banco de Vizcaya, which was one of Spain's largest banks. It was in the process of setting up an overseas branch in London and this would be the very first one for the bank. Despite my relative youth, at the age of 26 (and regardless of Kleinwort Benson's opinions), I was hired to run the credit department. Among other perks, I was promised regular business travel to Madrid as well as subsidised holiday travel to a hotel owned by the bank in southern Spain. I considered this a definite plus. I had travelled to Europe quite a bit, but always on holiday and not for work, and I had also spent my first summer break from university with my aunt and uncle in Madrid, which I loved. I saw the new job as my opportunity to do something very different while having affordable holidays with my wife and young children.

It started out pretty well. I did do some traveling, and lived in Madrid for about three months, working at the head office. This was in the days of General Franco, when Spain was not under martial law but it still a militarised kind of governance with a suspension of civil liberties. The Guardia Civil, a higher authority than the police, were obvious on the streets, more arrogant and brutal. They played a central role in maintaining the state control that was central to Franco's Madrid, but I did not feel repressed in any way. It turned out to be a short-term assignment but it really got me hooked on international business travel and its associated lifestyle, as well as the challenges associated with putting together syndicated loans. Syndicated loans were often used to put together amounts needed by a borrower which exceeded the legal lending limit of any one bank, or just to share risk. The lead bank would agree a term sheet with a borrower and then syndicate the loan out to a group of banks. For example, I was assigned to be part of a team which arranged a syndicated loan for over US$100 million for RENFE, Spain's state-owned railway. And I also very much enjoyed working in a different country with different work habits and a new lifestyle. This was clearly not Saddleworth.

In Spain, we started at 8 AM in the morning and worked through to 3 PM. I used to enjoy strolling down the lovely Paseo de La Castellana and past the Bernabeu Stadium which was across from my hotel in Plaza Cuzco. Our banking team rotated the work involved on projects so that small groups of usually two or three people could go out for coffee and churros mid-morning. At 3 PM, most of the staff went home for lunch (of course, by that time I was ravenous) and I was often invited to join one family or another. Sometimes, I would go to a restaurant with the guys I was working with. It was all great and I loved the Spanish food. After lunch, it was of course siesta time, which could be very long, or quite short if we had some urgent issues to deal with in the office. We would then regroup for drinks and tapas around 7 PM. I think I enjoyed the evenings the most. Dinner was at 10 PM and then we would go off to various bars around the city and stay out until the wee hours of the morning.

I remember one of my work colleagues saying to me, "If you

don't go back to England soon, I am sure we will have to send you back in a box."

Sadly, it all ended rather quickly. Not too long after I was hired to help set up the London branch of Banco de Vizcaya, the Bank of Spain put a restriction on overseas lending by Spanish banks. Banco de Vizcaya's obviously grandiose dream of building an active branch in London came crashing to the ground. I asked about being transferred to Spain on a permanent basis, but it transpired that that was not an option, the branch manager would not permit it. In addition, even if I had been assigned to Spain, the work would have been solely within Spain because of the restrictions on overseas lending. In other words, it would be just like any other domestic banking job with the exception of being posted somewhere in Spain instead of London.

We did, however, enjoy a two-week holiday at the bank's staff hotel just outside Alicante. My wife, two children and I were actually given a hotel booking for a month, but my holiday allowance only allowed for two weeks. So off we flew to Alicante and we were the first foreigners to stay in the hotel. Two significant events happened during our stay. The first was the death of Generalissimo Franco in November 1975, and the second was my daughter Claire taking her first steps. I have to say that this was the cheapest holiday I have ever had. In fact, I made on it—the bank paid a travel stipend on a per km basis and the hotel was heavily subsidised, so I ended up receiving an extra payment to settle accounts.

Shortly after this, on a cold winter's day back in London I got a call from the same recruiter in London who had found me my last two jobs. He looking to recruit me for a consortium owned by banks from Norway, Sweden, Finland and Denmark called Nordic Bank, and I was invited to the bank's humble offices in Mincing Lane, just round the corner from 20 Fenchurch Street where I had started my career and close to Leadenhall market and Lloyds of London. I was interviewed by the HR Director who questioned me about my career to date, my work ethic, and particularly my experience in the areas of credit analysis, business development and syndicated loans. A few days later I was invited to lunch in a club in Leadenhall market with the HR Director, the Deputy Chairman and my boss-to-be Ken Buchanan, whose initials were KGB. A few days later, I received an offer to take on a managerial role as head of Credit appraisal, and head of UK business development at a good salary of almost GBP 7,000 per annum, a loan to fund the purchase of an annual rail ticket of GBP 136 per annum, to cover my commutes between home and office, and a subsidised mortgage. I immediately jumped at it and started working there in 1976. And this was where I truly started my banking career. The lavish offices and dining rooms of Kleinwort Benson and Western American Bank that I had come to enjoy were in the past, but the job catapulted me into a world of international travel, problem-solving, and business sleuthing that would shape my career and impact my view of the world for years to come.

Nordic Bank at the time, was fairly new and had fewer than a hundred employees. The staff were mainly English, but each of the shareholder banks—one from each of the Nordic countries (Den Norske Bank, Svenska Handelsbanken, Kansallis Osake Pankii, Copenhagen Handelsbank)—had a desk with a native in place. There was also an active ship financing department. In less than three weeks, I received my first overseas assignment. I got called into KGB's office where he explained that one of the bank's customers, a Swedish company that was manufacturing photo posters in a facility in Frankfurt, was having trouble repaying a loan. I was instructed to find out what the problem was and report back. I spoke terrible German and not a word of

Swedish, but I booked a three-day business trip to Frankfurt in West Germany, my very first solo business venture abroad.

I checked into the iconic Frankfurter Hof Hotel, rich in history and classic architecture. This was luxury on a level to which I was not accustomed, but the elegance and opulence were super enjoyable. However, being alone and on my first trip for the bank, I was frugal with my expenses, and happily dug into the "real local food" of sausages, pork knuckles and schnitzel washed down with some beer, of course. It was only later that I developed my taste for good wine.

I wanted to get my first assignment right, so I took my time to research and investigate the situation. One of the reasons the Swedish company had set up its operations in Frankfurt was that labor there was cheaper than back home, but I smelled trouble right from the start. I didn't accept the company manager's surface-level explanations, nor did I rely on any pre-existing reports other than to use them to ask more detailed questions. I dug as deep as I could and continually asked questions about what was going on while observing the company's day-to-day operations. After three days, I was questioning the overall viability of the business and expressed this in a detailed report to my bosses when I returned to London. I advised the bank to not lend the company any more money and my advice was accepted. In that way, I established my first bona fides as a troubleshooter who could assess difficult situations and offer valuable insights. I became Nordic Bank's traveling problem solver and rarely spent more than three weeks in the London office in one stretch. I was constantly on the move to locations and countries around the world.

My assignments took me from London to Singapore to Hong Kong, Australia, where the bank had offices, and Saudi Arabia, Bahrain, the United States, South America, and Iceland for loan negotiations, signings, supporting clients or looking for new business. The list went on and on and the flights were endless. In some cases, it was to relieve a colleague. In other cases, it was to check on a particular loan or issues within an overseas unit. But the core part of the job was to keep my wits about me, to spot new opportunities to develop business deals, and to identify any problems with the loans we had out in the market or in the offices I visited. In a way, I was sometimes an undercover auditor, though I had no actual auditing credentials. I was more of an internal troubleshooter for Nordic Bank as well as a risk management specialist. Others would perhaps call me a financial spy, and I am sure that many of the managers of the offices I visited were more than wary of me.

I had a fairly simple technique for doing this job. I never arrived at a company with a clipboard or a specific list of questions. Instead, I relied on my ability to engage in conversations with staff, observe the office dynamics, and ask good questions that occurred to me on the fly. Above all else, I became a good listener. In this way, I could gather high quality intelligence on a situation without raising too many red flags within the operation under scrutiny. The office staff would freely share their thoughts and opinions, without realising they were actually providing me with quality information about the health of their company operations.

There was nothing easy about this job. Sure, I loved the travel and getting to network with people from all walks of life and in all parts of the world. But I was also put into some tough situations precisely because I had become quite good at ferreting out problems within various companies that Nordic Bank had helped to finance and the operations in their different offices. For example, on my first trip to Asia in late December 1977, I travelled to Singapore to relieve a manager who was going on home leave for a month. I was quite excited to be given the opportunity to see a new part of the world. The excitement turned to frustration very quickly after I landed at the Payer Labar Airport. The now famous Changi Airport was still under construction at the time (it opened in 1981). After disembarking from the plane, I had to wait ninety minutes for a taxi in a long queue, sweating a like the proverbial pig. It was a far cry from the cold, damp and wet London that I had left behind. Thankfully Changi airport today is one of the world's most efficient and taxi queues are seldomly visible. I spent my first few days in the Goodwood Park Hotel before moving to the house of the manager I was covering for just off Bukit Timah Road.

The Nordic Bank office in Singapore was on Shenton Way which in those days, before extensive land reclamations took place, was just across from the waterfront. There were fewer than thirty people working in the office, so it was easy to get to know everyone. It was run by a Swedish guy and the number two person was Norwegian. I was constantly invited out for lunch and dinner on the weekends. Our local lunches were often at the Lau Pa Sat Market, which offered a host of local dishes including tantalising Malay and Chinese specialties. It was such a vibrant scene full of odours unfamiliar to me and it did not take long for me to fall in love with the food. I loved the seafood restaurants on East Coast Road and the food centre at Newton Circus. My weekends were a mixture of visits to the Dutch or Tanglin club and trips over the causeway into Malaysia for lunch at a little fishing village called Kuk Up.

While I was on assignment in Singapore, I was called to Hong Kong. The bank was in the process of setting up a Deposit Taking Company and there were some concerns about the person who had been appointed as the MD. I was sent to check out some issues that had not been formally reported. At first, I thought it was a more general matter of simply following up on something that had not been correctly reported on or in a timely fashion. However, it turned out to be much more complicated. My inquiries led to the discovery that the MD was running a Jaguar through the banks books in addition to the car he had been allocated, a high end Granada, There were also staff and security issues plus constant absences when he could usually be found in the bar at the Mandarin Hotel. The trip turned into a major intervention with the removal of the Managing Director and me temporarily taking over the business. Whether this was fortunate or unfortunate, the 'temporary situation' lasted much longer than planned. I became the acting MD until a designated person could take over, which did not occur until a year later, in January 1979.

I was immediately struck by how amazing Hong Kong was. It had such a buzz. My first flight into Hong Kong was into the old Kai Tak Airport in the middle of the city, the runway stretching out into the harbour. It was a landing that I marvelled about for years to come. The plane flew in seemingly between the apartment buildings. It felt so close that you could almost see what people were watching on TV before the plane made a very sharp bank right to align with the runway. As the engines went into reverse thrust careering towards the sea, you got hit by the smell of the fragrant harbour (Hong Kong in English means just that, 'Fragrant Harbour'). This was so distinctive that if someone took you on a blindfolded mystery tour with no announcements, you would know just by the smell that you had landed in Hong Kong.

In those days, there was only one tunnel to cross the harbour and most people still used the famous cross-harbour ferries. There was no MTR subway, but that was starting construction, and while I was there half the pavements in the Central business district were raised wooden platforms covering the construction below.

I stayed in the Mandarin Hotel, one of the great hotels of the Far East, and was particularly attracted to the Captains Bar, just off the lobby. Moreover, our office was on Connaught Road so it was only a five-minute walk to work, which was heaven after my long commutes in London, an hour and a half each way. Hong Kong was far more vibrant, crowded and intense than Singapore. It offered lots of night life and great food options, including some of my favourites still exist today, like the New American in Wanchai, famous for its Peking duck, and the Peking Garden in Alexandra House with its noodle-making show. The Chinese restaurants around D'Aguilar Street and the seafood restaurants on the island of Lamma were sublime. Sometimes in the evening and at weekends, we would hire a junk and sail out into the South China Sea. I made several lasting friendships in those weeks, mainly bankers and lawyers, but also some more casual acquaintances in the bars and restaurants of Central and Stanley Market.

During that first stay in Hong Kong, I was able to make a weekend trip to Taipei, where I stayed at the famous Grand Hotel. Back in those days, you could walk across paddy fields from the hotel to get into town. I felt quite apprehensive about traveling alone in Taipei because there was very little English spoken and all the street signs were in Chinese. Rather than exploring the city on my own, I took a guided tour. The National Museum was amazing with all the artefacts and treasures brought over from Mainland China. I also had first experience of eating snake, which was of course killed in front of me before it was cooked.

Things were not always straight forward for me in those Hong Kong days, but life was never dull. One Friday night, for example, not long after I had moved into an apartment in the

Mid-Levels, I returned home late after having had dinner with clients at the then iconic Repulse Bay Hotel and was surprised to find the Amah (a live-in maid) still awake and waiting for me.

"Oh sir," she said. "You must call your boss London quickie quickie urgent."

I immediately picked up the phone and called KGB in London.

"We have another great opportunity for you, Atkinson," he said. "It's a special assignment. We need you in the Maldives as soon as possible." The Bank had made a loan to a Lebanese businessman to support the purchase of fish freezing equipment from Alfa Laval, a client of the bank.

"Oh!" I replied. "Can you tell me whether I fly east or west because, to be honest, I have no idea where the Maldives actually are."

He suggested that I might try flying west. Since Saturday was a working morning in Hong Kong, I was able to contact my friendly travel agent and determined that to get to the Maldives I had to go through Sri Lanka and that there was a flight leaving Hong Kong that evening from Tokyo, bound for Sri Lanka and beyond. A seat was booked together with a room in an exotic sounding hotel in Colombo called the Browns Beach Hotel. I then had to go to the doctors to get yellow fever injections and was warned not to touch the local water and only to drink soda from a can and even to use that for brushing my teeth. So off I went on another journey into the unknown. The flight was great. It was a British Airways flight and there was a small group of expats on board who managed to set up a galley party at the back of the plane.

By the time I cleared immigration and customs in Colombo, it was past 2:00 AM. It took a while to find my hotel and I had to wake up the reception staff to check in and get my room key. Completely exhausted, I walked into my room and flopped onto the bed only to find out that the mattress was less than half an inch thick underneath which was on a board that almost broke my back. I had the most uncomfortable night of sleep that one can imagine after a fairly long journey. In the morning, my mission was to find a local travel agent to handle the vagaries of booking a flight to the Maldives. I left my room and, walking across the garden to the hotel reception area, I saw something that made me think I was dreaming. I opened and closed my eyes several times, but still standing there, right in front of me with his trunk swinging back and forth, was an elephant. Right there in the middle of the hotel garden! An unusual site for someone used to working in London and Hong Kong.

With the help of a local travel agent, I managed to get a flight to the Maldives for the following day. I set off for what I thought was going to be a two-day journey, but I had no such luck. Upon arrival to the Maldives, I checked into the government guest house in Male (another dull affair) and then went to the office of the Ministry of Justice to request a meeting with the Minister. The people in the office looked at me as though I had landed from the moon. They took note of my request, asked for confirmation that I was staying at the government guest house and then told me to go back to my room and wait. Three days later, they called me and said the Minister would see me on Friday, which was the last working day of the week and two days away. My heart sank at the thought of spending two more days in a dumpy guesthouse, but what could I do? On Friday, I arrived at the Minister's office at the appointed time only to be told that there had been a coup d'etat a few weeks before and that the new ministry did not recognise any arrangement approved or agreed to by the previous government. They appeared neither interested nor willing to listen to my case.

However, at the very least, I had had a meeting and I could

now leave and report back to my bosses on the situation. I can't remember if I told them that the place was quite boring, but it was. In the week I was there, I learned that the island was very small and I was able to walk around it entirely in about 30 minutes. The only real thing of interest was watching the tuna boat catches being brought ashore in the late afternoon. Our client had the idea of setting up freezing stations at various places around the islands so the small boats could drop off their catches and he would freeze and wait until there were enough tuna to fill a container which he would then ship out. At that time, Maldives only had one tourist resort island which I did visit but just for an afternoon on a speed boat which made for a scary return in the dark.

I returned to Sri Lanka and met some lawyers who I appointed to represent us on the Maldives issue, and then flew off back to Hong Kong. It was not the best result that I ever had from such a trip, but at least I had had a new experience, and had re-learned the lesson that traveling was not always luxury, fine food, and drinks.

My posting to Singapore with the extended 'side trip' to Hong Kong changed how I was perceived within the bank. I had earned a reputation as a troubleshooter, someone who had a keen eye for ferreting out problems and finding solutions. But this was a double-edged sword. Whenever and wherever around the world I showed up for a visit, no matter how innocent, the office staff would greet me with a mixture of respect and apprehension. I was still in my early thirties, but I was being placed into quite high positions of power and influence because of my track record, my skill set and the trust my boss placed in me.

But then again, sometimes even the simplest things escaped me. For example, on my very first trip to Seoul, South Korea in October 1978, I wore lightweight autumn clothes that were perfect for Hong Kong, but were practically useless in what felt, when I exited Seoul airport, like the frozen tundra of Siberia. It was a business development trip and totally unchartered territory for me. I should have done some research, but there were not many sources one could search at that time. Seoul in 1978 was not the gleaming metropolis of K-pop and Samsung that exists today. The entire capital city boasted a grand total of only two international hotels – the Lotte and the newly opened Hyatt on what was known locally as Bunker Hill. With the Lotte fully booked, I opted for the Hyatt, blissfully unaware of what lay ahead.

Due to the shock administered to me by Mother Nature, my first order of business was not banking but simple basic survival. I went on an emergency shopping expedition to Itaewon market near the US army base just a five-minute walk down the hill from the Hyatt. Upon arrival, I deployed my newly acquired negotiation skills, learned in Stanley Market in Hong Kong, for the procurement of a sweater and warm jacket at non-tourist prices.

Communication proved to be the next hurdle. The Hyatt, despite being new, had mercifully hired some English-speaking staff who I enlisted to help me by writing addresses in Korean for taxi drivers. This seemingly simple task concealed a maddening quirk of Seoul's urban planning. As I later learned, the buildings were numbered in the order they had been constructed, not by their position on the street. No doubt, I irritated and confused my non-English speaking taxi driver as I tried to instruct him to find building #2 and eventually figured out that it was between buildings #147 and #53.

Evening brought yet another surprise in the form of a 10 o'clock curfew, a concept utterly foreign to me, having become accustomed to living in cities that never sleep. Not only did this mean racing back to the hotel by 10 PM, but it also meant that anyone inside the hotel at curfew was required to stay until morning, whether they had a room or not. The presence of a nightclub within the hotel created what I can only describe as an "interesting" overnight situation.

The pièce de résistance of cultural shocks occurred on the second day. While navigating Seoul's underground shopping centre labyrinth, I was suddenly engulfed by what appeared to be the Apocalypse. Air raid sirens blared through the tunnels as people rushed about with stretchers carrying "injured" victims. For a young man whose greatest workplace stress had previously been meeting quarterly targets, I found myself in what appeared to be the opening scene of Red Dawn: Seoul Edition. It was pretty terrifying.

Later, at the meeting which I arrived at late and apologetic, my Korean hosts casually explained that this was merely a routine drill to prepare for a possible North Korean invasion. This was information that would have been tremendously helpful approximately two hours earlier and would have saved me a lot of stress.

My final cultural revelation came in the form of mandatory Sunday overtime work shifts because the country had fallen behind on its export targets. This compulsory practice, which would have sent Western labor unions into apoplectic fits, was apparently accepted without complaint by Koreans in 1978. It was part of the Korean work ethic, and it helps explain how Seoul was able to transform itself in just a few decades from an isolated city with just two decent hotels in 1978 to a global powerhouse.

My trouble-shooting skills were again called upon in early 1983, this time in Australia. I had just returned from a business development trip to South America including Argentina, Brazil, Venezuela and Mexico, when I was asked to fly to Sydney to participate in meetings about a loan that was in trouble. The creditors, including Nordic Bank, had made a substantial loan to International Harvester, and the company had defaulted on the loan. At the time, Australia was experiencing a severe drought, which had devastated the agricultural sector. Nordic Bank was in for about $5 to $10 million, which exposed us to significant risk. This was the start of a six-week visit Down Under that would expose me to another culture and different work ethics.

The creditors meetings were held in Melbourne whereas our office, as well as some of the other banks' offices, were in Sydney. This meant travelling to Melbourne early Monday morning and returning late Friday afternoon. Everything was casual and laid back, but it was clear that the lawyers were running the meetings and not the bankers whose money was on the line. I really had not travelled all that way just to hear lawyers arguing over split infinitives, so I suggested that the banks should run the meeting instead, and the lawyers, who should have been there simply to document what the lenders agreed to, immediately saw me as an enemy. In addition, the representatives of major Australian retail banks at the table tagged me as an upstart "pom", an inconvenient Englishman. At the end of the second week of meetings, I suggested to the Sydney-based bankers that maybe we should meet on Saturday mornings in order to agree on strategy ahead of the coming weeks of creditor meetings. I also wanted to gain a better understanding of their thinking on how to resolve the problem. There was more than a little reluctance about coming into work on a Saturday, but they agreed. Of course, being a London banker, I arrived at the "meeting" in suit and tie and walked into an office where everyone was dressed in shorts and t-shirts, with thongs on their feet! I was embarrassed, but managed to humour my way through the situation, which gradually became easier as everyone was drinking wine and beer. Later on, one of the guys invited me to go sailing in Sydney harbour the following day (Sunday). The meetings there and in Melbourne happily ended with a result that was favourable to the lenders, of which Nordic bank was one. But before leaving London for Sydney, I had been instructed to "sniff around the office a little bit." This was becoming one of the key tasks because of my ability to find and solve problems. In the Australia case, my investigation led to a significant leadership change that essentially mirrored what had happened in Hong Kong. This pattern of uncovering issues and catalysing leadership changes became a recurring theme in my career with Nordic Bank.

I loved Sydney, the harbour, and the wonderful fresh seafood. Doyles restaurant at Watsons Bay, looking back to the Sydney Harbour Bridge, remains a favourite of mine to this day. Back in 1983 it was a BYO, meaning alcohol was not served by the restaurant and had to be brought in by customers. I was staying at the Regent Hotel close to the Bridge and right on the water, and often wandered around the oldest section of the city nearby, the "Rocks", visiting the many little bars and restaurants in the buildings dating back to not long after Sydney was founded in 1788. Melbourne was totally different type of city, and in some ways like London, at least in terms of its changeable weather. The city at that time had not been really been connected to its own stretch of water, the Yarra River, but it has a totally different feeling now with many wonderful waterfront restaurants.

To maintain my sanity and to preserve and build friendships, I had to work on separating business and friendship. This is not easy. It's easy to claim to be professionally detached, but my involvement could often lead to unpleasant outcomes for some people. Sometimes this included removing a person from his/her job which could result in significant career setbacks. Of course, I never held any grudges and I am not a vindictive person, but I did have to give frank appraisals and report what was going on as accurately as I could. That was the job. If I wanted to succeed as an international banker, I had to make tough calls without being swayed by personal sympathies or office politics, and that meant I often found myself in the uncomfortable position of being resented. I also know that while I may have felt I was being objective and professional, the people impacted felt very differently. It hurts to get fired.

I often felt I was on an ethical tightrope. My work was essential to maintain the bank's financial health and integrity. By identifying problems early and recommending corrective actions, I was protecting the bank's interests, potentially saving it from significant losses and reputational damage. On the other hand, the covert nature of how I went about my work raised questions about transparency and trust within the organisation. Employees who spoke freely to me, believing that I was just another colleague, might feel betrayed upon learning of my true role, and there was a human cost involved. The derailed careers and tarnished reputations weighed on me. But I am pleased that I maintained long lasting relationships with staff in both the Hong Kong and Australian offices of Nordic Bank, long after I had left to set up my own business.

One of my personal challenges, and a point of criticism from others, was that I was doing this work when I was relatively young compared to others around me. I was still in my early thirties. I had shot up the corporate ladder to become a globe-trotting business developer, financial "detective," and loan negotiator thanks to the support of my boss Ken Buchanan. It was a testament to my adaptability and acumen, and it shaped not only my career but also the trajectory of Nordic Bank's international operations.

In hindsight, there was nothing novel about my techniques.

I was an active listener, a careful observer, and I had the gift of being able to connect disparate pieces of information in a manner that revealed the larger picture. This was a useful skill in the often-opaque environment of international finance in the late 20th century, where problems could easily be concealed across borders and cultural divides. Perhaps my methods would raise eyebrows in today's more transparent corporate environment, but that wasn't the case back in the 1970s and '80s. I sometimes think back on my early career at Nordic Bank and it feels like a John Grisham-style financial thriller. There was international intrigue, high-stakes decision making, and the constant challenge of uncovering the truth behind balance sheets and boardroom smiles. But instead of a financial thriller, I have this memoir. I hope it offers a glimpse into the hidden workings of international banking and the sometimes-invisible hands that guide the fate of global financial institutions. I know I learned a lot from this, my first "real job" in banking.

4

BEHIND THE IRON CURTAIN

By the time 1979 rolled around and I returned to my post in Nordic Bank London, I was beginning to get a handle on what it meant to be an international banker. There were a few things to always be ready for and be aware of. First, my office phone could ring at any time and on any given day with marching orders to help solve a problem or save a banking deal somewhere in Europe, Asia, North America, or really anywhere in the world. With international finance deals, it was the norm that issues would come up and I was often the one sent to figure it all out and find a solution. Second, because of that first point, I made sure I always had my passport with me. In fact, I had two of them, and I could head for the airport at a moment's notice. Third, I made a point of always saying 'Yes' to any and all projects, no matter how complicated they seemed or how little background information I had on the deal, the country, the culture, the partners, the whatever. I had a "Yeah, why not? I'll give it a shot" attitude that was not too common for someone my age, much less for someone working in finance. I guess I trusted myself enough to believe that I would find a solution and get the deal done no matter what obstacles I was going to face, with the knowledge that my boss was always there to back me up.

By the late 1970s, this attitude had elevated me to a kind of 'rising star' status within Nordic Bank. My office was in the bustling financial district of London, I was young, ambitious, and getting good at my job. Perhaps for this reason, my desk phone rang in February 1979, shortly after I returned from my posting in Hong Kong. It was the manager of the Finnish Desk in Nordic's London office.

"Ken, I've got a hotel project in Leningrad," the voice crackled through the receiver. "Two Finnish construction companies are involved, and we need to figure out how to finance this through the private sector. Can you help?"

My first thought was, "Leningrad? The one in the USSR?" Surely, he wasn't referring to THAT Leningrad? In the late 1970s, financing a project in the Soviet Union with Western capital was virtually unheard of. No one did it because no one outside of the Eastern Bloc knew how or if such projects could be done. Who would guarantee such a deal? How would the debt be paid off? How would profits, if there were any, be extracted? The only loan deals bridging the Iron Curtain that had been done were bank-to-bank with the USSR's Bank for Foreign Trade and there had been very few of them.

My head was exploding with questions because the fact was that such a venture had never been done before. The better move would no doubt have been to stick with deals in Western Europe or North America, where there was transparency and a well-trodden path to success. Leningrad? Was this Finn crazy? Why should I put my head on the line for such an inherently risky project?

"Of course I can help," I replied without another thought. Little did I know that I had just catapulted myself into a whirlwind of international intrigue, high-stakes negotiations, and encounters with some of the most colourful characters of the Cold War.

Life in the Soviet Union of the 1970s was socially stable, but economically stagnant. The majority of citizens had access to basic services such as healthcare, education, and subsidised housing. But there were constant scarcities and few personal freedoms. There was basically no unemployment although it's not likely that a government salary would make anyone, at least not regular citizens, rich. The media was strictly controlled, and its purpose was to support the status quo and extoll the virtues of the Communist Party which was fully in charge. The government and the Party, which were effectively one in the same, controlled everything. This definitively included the financing and construction of a luxury hotel with foreign developers from the West.

Leonid Brezhnev, the General Secretary of the Communist Party of the Union of Soviet Socialist Republics (USSR), was nearing the end of his 18-year tenure (1964 to 1982). He was in poor health, but managed to stay in power until the very end, dying like Joseph Stalin while still in power. He became the Soviet leader after a carefully orchestrated coup toppled Nikita Khrushchev, who had managed to grab power after Stalin's death in 1953.

By the late 1970s, when I arrived, the Soviet economy was struggling due to inefficiencies, government corruption, and a heavy focus on military spending during the Cold War. Good quality consumer goods, in fact quality goods of any kind, were in short supply. There were often long lines for basic food supplies. Travel outside of the Soviet Union by Soviet citizens was strictly controlled, as was the import of outside products such as books, movies, and other items that could have an influence on people. In short, the Soviet Union of the late 1970s and early 1980s was in decline. The era of '*glasnost*' (political openness) and '*perestroika*' (economic restructuring) under the leadership of Mikhail Gorbachev was nearly 10 years away.

Given all these issues and trends, it was hard to imagine that there was any kind of pent up demand for a foreign-invested hotel in the city of Leningrad in the year 1979, although it was being built partly with the 1980 Moscow Olympic Games in mind. I had many questions buzzing around in my head, including who was such a hotel for, how much would it cost to build, what would the room rate be, would guests pay in rubles or in dollars, could the hotel owners repatriate profits, if there turned out to be any, either in rubles or dollars? And how could such a project get any of the kind of loan guarantees that Western banks would typically demand of any property project built anywhere else in the world? My job was to try and find the answers to these seemingly unanswerable questions.

Within days, I was on a plane to Helsinki, the first stop on what would become a fascinating globe-trotting adventure. In the Finnish capital, I met with representatives of the Finnish Export Credit agency (FEC) and the Finnish Export Guarantee Board (FEGB) together with the representatives of our Finnish shareholder, Kansallis Osake Pankki, and the Country desk manager from Nordic Bank. The construction companies, Poulimatka (Polar Rakennus Oy) and Lemminkäinen, were also present, along with a prominent figure in Finland's real estate industry at the time named Harry Hinteka.

As we brainstormed ways to structure the deal, my mind raced with possibilities. The biggest challenge was how to get such a project in the Soviet Union financed when Western government institutions were prohibited from lending directly to entities behind the Iron Curtain.

After many hours of discussion, we came up with an idea that had never been tried before. The Finnish export Credit agency would lend the money to Nordic Bank in London, which would then on-lend it to the project in Leningrad. To mitigate the risk, Nordic Bank would secure a guarantee from the Finnish Export Guarantee Board, and also a guarantee from the Bank for Foreign Trade of the USSR. This was my first workaround to get a project financed in a country like the Soviet Union, and it was an approach would gradually begin to allow for East-West financial cooperation. But at that time, it was just an idea, completely untested.

Upon my return to London, I was introduced to the hotel project's promoter, a fascinating character named Cyrus Eaton Jr, who was based in Cleveland Ohio, a place I later visited several times. His father was a contemporary of, and had been a business partner with Armand Hammer, the American industrialist who had gained fame for his dealings with the Soviet Union, from the 1920s through the 1970s. Back then, the international press called Hammer "Lenin's Chosen Capitalist." Eaton, possibly through his Hammer connection, had been granted a piece of land in Leningrad's Nevsky Prospekt which he planned to use to build the hotel. This was in replacement for a piece of land he had previously been granted in Moscow, which had been determined to be unsuitable. Rumour had it that it was too close to the KGB's headquarters.

As I delved deeper into the project, I found himself working closely with Clara Reece, who was Eaton's formidable second-in-command. Clara, a Hungarian refugee who had fled to the United States when she was 16 years old, was a force to be reckoned with. Her understanding of the Eastern Bloc proved invaluable, but her demanding nature often tested my patience. So, too, did her impetuousness. Like the day she called me out of the blue with news that would change my life.

"I want you on a flight tomorrow morning to Moscow," she virtually barked at me over the phone. "Aeroflot. Don't worry about hotels or visas. I'll take care of everything."

My protests and concerns about the need for visas and my reluctance to fly Aeroflot fell on deaf ears. Clara assured me that my visa would be arranged on arrival which I had a hard time believing.

The next few days were quite a whirlwind and certainly confirmed my desire never ever to travel by Aeroflot. I was also worried before we landed about whether the "visa on arrival" service would work, not to mention freezing to death before we actually got there even though I was traveling First Class. The air hostesses ignored us, and the inside of the plane was pretty drab verging on hostile, with no real First Class comforts and crucially no blankets.

We landed in Moscow at Sheremetyevo airport and I was met by people from the travel service who did indeed have my visa and who escorted me through the usual dour immigration process into a waiting car, a huge limousine. The drive into Moscow seemed long, but fortunately there was not much in the way of traffic and in fact, the journey was only about 18 miles and took less than 30 minutes. I remember we drove past a long line of metal crosses just outside of the city which I later learned marked the line that the German army had reached during their attack on Moscow during World War II.

Red Square Moscow 1979

The hotel I was shown into was huge and relatively modern. It featured a big conference centre where they were starting to hold concerts by international music acts. The most unusual feature of the hotel were several burly women who looked like sumo wrestlers on each floor. They oversaw who came in and out of the rooms. Of course, they totally controlled the room keys. I would not have liked to have met one of them in the dark!

Anyway, I had made it to Moscow. That evening, Clara summoned me to dinner at the National Hotel, the crown jewel of Moscow's hospitality scene at the time. I was excited about this especially after perusing the extensive menu. I couldn't wait to start ordering, but I quickly got my first lesson in what life was like in Moscow in the late 1970s. Every dish that I ordered, or asked for, received a firm "*Nyet*" (no) from the waiter. Presumably, they had run out of or had never had that particular dish in the first place. The menu was in fact purely for show. In the end, the "Grand Feast" that I had envisioned consisted of borscht soup, a small jar of caviar for each of us, blinis, and a bottle of vodka. Clara matched me drink for drink with the vodka. She also taught me another lesson about life in Moscow and Russian hospitality. You had better be able to drink, and you should drink vodka neat and ice cold which helps reduce the risk of a hangover. To my amazement, Clara ordered another half bottle of vodka as we talked about the deal we were there to work on and how to get it done.

The next few weeks were a series of meetings with representatives of the Bank for Foreign Trade of the USSR. Its role was to provide a guarantee to Nordic Bank for the loan. All our meetings were in Moscow, and it seemed like a visit to the site in Leningrad was not going to be possible, not that I was really pushing for one because I was deathly afraid of taking a domestic flight on Aeroflot. We stayed in Moscow and just kept on talking.

This was also one of the first deals that I put together with my go-to lawyer John East of the law firm Clifford Chance, and what a journey we had! At one meeting, coffee was served from a jug placed in the middle of the table, and John whispered to me to be careful because it was probably laced with vodka. It was, which was too bad because the coffee smelt great. After three rounds of meetings, with and without vodka-laced coffee, our efforts paid off with a final deal which came together in July 1979.

Of course, there were more meetings after the deal was sealed. In one of them, I remember being at a loss for words when the Russian lawyer representing the Bank for Foreign Trade asked about the force majeure provision and John used war as an example. The lawyer then asked if that was a threat or a promise. I handed that question off to John. On another occasion, the same Russian lawyer stood up and started ranting once again about some of the fairly standard legal language we required in the agreement. I started to stand up to respond, but John stamped on my foot and I sat down again. The Russian lawyer kept going on and on how preposterous the provisions were, how his bank had never issued such a legal opinion before, and so on. John feigned interest as he let the storm blow over and then casually and quietly responded by saying, "That is very interesting as I was the lawyer for the recent Citibank syndicated loan that was signed a few weeks ago. This opinion is exactly the same as that one." To my recollection, the Citibank loan was the first such Western loan made to the USSR. Not surprisingly, that particular lawyer never appeared again at any future meetings.

As for the hotel project itself, the Pulkovskya Hotel, in what is now once again St. Petersburg, stands as a testament to my time in Eastern Europe. It later came under the management of the Radisson Group, and one of the people with whom I worked in Beijing and who also signed the contract for my first project in Vietnam in 1989, Arild Hovland, became the Radisson's Business Development Director for Soviet Union. He has a bar named after him in the Pulkovskya Hotel. I learned this from the General Manager of the Radisson Blu in Nha Trang who had previously served as a GM of the St. Petersburg hotel. Another

With John East and Ken Buchanan c 1980

'Small World' moment!

The hotel project was done, but I wasn't. It was not a case of one project and then back to London. If that had happened, I would have lived a very different life compared to what I actually ended up doing for much of the 1980s. Looking back on that pivotal year of 1979, I often marvel at how a single phone call had set me on a path that would define my banking career. With that first hotel project in Leningrad, I learned so many lessons. This included the importance of innovation, the power of perseverance, and the value of cross-cultural understanding. All of these have served me well throughout my career. The fall of the Berlin Wall was still ten years away, but I was already gathering together the tools and skills I needed to survive and to some extent thrive on the front lines of international finance. I was ready to take on the next challenge. Nordic Bank was ready as well, and the Soviet Union was but just one of several countries behind the Iron Curtain.

The Cold War was still very much ongoing in the early 1980s when I arrived in Warsaw, the capital of Poland, on a business trip for the bank. The city still bore the scars of World War II. Its streets were crowded with boxy Soviet-made cars and its economy was struggling under the weight of communist rule. I was there to put together another deal, but it nearly got derailed before I could even leave the airport. At the Polish passport control, the immigration officials found two passports in my briefcase. In the paranoid world of Cold War Eastern Europe, this was tantamount to declaring oneself a spy. I hadn't concealed it. Anyone who bothered to open my briefcase would have found it right away. I didn't really think about it. As it turns out, the immigration police didn't know what to do about a potential security threat of my having two passports. We were at a standoff.

I had an ace up my sleeve. Or at least, I thought I might have an ace up my sleeve. It was the phone number of the Finnish Commercial Attache to Poland. I was allowed to make a phone call so I called him and explained the situation.

"Don't worry, I'll be right down," he said.

The Attache arrived and began to smooth things over with the authorities. In the end, a compromise was reached. I was allowed into Poland, but there was a note in my passport stating that I had a second passport. This was actually important because when I left the country, after my business was concluded, they demanded that I produce the second passport. They wanted to make sure I hadn't sold it on the black market.

The saving grace was that I was booked into a relatively new hotel in the city centre called the Vittoria, which had a great nightclub in the basement. The champagne, the caviar, and all the "trimmings" were amazing and, at the black-market rate, they were also very cheap. The trick in some of these countries, such as Poland, was to exchange only the required amount of foreign currency into local currency. This had to take place at the airport and naturally the exchange rates were awful. I would exchange the absolute minimum amount, get a receipt, and then change more later on with taxi drivers and others at a much higher black-market rate. This enabled me to live the Life of Riley, but on the cheap. My bosses could never understand why my expenses were always so low. I would buy clothes for my kids in Poland, which were exceptionally cheap, as well as crystal glasses in Czechoslovakia. It was great.

Great, but not always easy during the Cold War. It seemed that each business trip into Eastern Europe required a delicate dance of diplomacy, nerves, and occasionally a bit of rule-bending. I had a front row seat on the details of daily life behind the Iron Curtain, where even the simplest tasks could require a surreal struggle to complete. For example, in Czechoslovakia, I arrived at the Intercontinental Hotel in Prague and thought I was all set. At the time, it was the only luxury hotel in the city. I had a confirmed booking and showed it to the front desk. However, they claimed to have no record of my reservation and told me the hotel was fully booked. I reverted to my master skill of polite persistence and refusing to say 'no' when I needed a 'yes' answer from the other side. I was there with a Finnish colleague.

"Okay then, if you don't have a room, I'm going have to sleep on the counter," I told them. "And my friend is going to sleep behind the counter."

Amazingly the hotel staff found a junior suite with one bed and a sofa couch. We flipped a coin for who got to sleep in the bed. He did!

These hotel hijinks were just part of the tapestry of doing business during the Cold War. My work took me all over Eastern Europe. I worked on business deals in Poland, East Germany, Czechoslovakia, Bulgaria and Yugoslavia, as well as in the USSR. I was constantly on the move. Each country presented its own unique challenges and bizarre encounters. In East Germany, I stayed a couple of times in a very new hotel called the Palast in East Berlin. The hotel was about 500 meters away from the infamous Checkpoint Charlie. My usual preference, however, was to stay in West Berlin and navigate Check Point Charlie in the morning by walking to my meetings in East Berlin with just my briefcase. The Palast Hotel offered basic comforts, but nothing that could be described as luxury. On my first stay there, I walked to the hotel after passing through Checkpoint Charlie. It was a cold and dark autumn evening and there were no taxis. I had a map and knew it was a straight line from the checkpoint so I basically just followed my nose, lugging my suitcase and briefcase. In those days, luggage didn't come with wheels.

At night, there was nothing to do and the street lights were rare and dim. Dark, cold, and grim was the norm. The whole idea of doing business with 'The East' was fraught with tension and paranoia. My meetings with the Deutsche Aussenhandelsbank, just a hundred meters from the Brandenburg Gate, were exercises in careful diplomacy and constant vigilance. I'm sure the conversations were bugged and I sometimes made fun of the scenario by talking with a flower pot and saying something like, "Good morning flowerpot. I know you're listening to me."

I had no choice, really, but to make as much fun as I could of a tough situation. Even in situations that could potentially be dangerous, I would tend to choose humour rather than fear. For example, I had another immigration run-in with Russian officials while a trip to the Soviet Union. The immigration official wouldn't let me out because he said my face in real life didn't look like the face in my passport. I assured them that it was me in person and me in the passport and that I had an entry stamp in my passport.

"I don't think that's you," he said.

"Yeah, I am a bit older now, but that is me," I said. "Please, trust me. It is me."

Though I tried to joke my way through such situations, they were highly stressful. This particular immigration official could have easily refused me exit out of the Soviet Union simply because he believed that the photo in my passport wasn't me. I encountered several of these incidents and I often wondered if I would get stuck in some Eastern European country during the Cold War because I was "doing business."

Customs, flights, immigration, and hotels were just some of the challenges. After getting into a country and checking into a hotel, the "doing business" part of the deal featured an entirely different set of frustrations and stresses. I was trying to help a range of Western companies figure out how to do business in

Eastern Europe, but there was a sharp learning curve on my side. A typical deal involved a paper mill project in Poland where I was acting for a Swedish client with financing guaranteed by Bank Handlowy, the Polish foreign trade bank. It was a complicated deal that resulted in very late nights, lots of negotiations, and lots and lots of vodka. This was typical of most of the deals in those days – lots of talking and lots of vodka.

What was also typical was how things just rolled over, day after day, without any apparent progress. It was like the Bill Murray movie 'Groundhog Day.' During the course of a day, we would agree on various issues and papers would be drawn up for signing on the following day. The next morning, it was the previous day had not happened at all and the details had never been discussed, we had to start over again from scratch. That was the way things were, and it was important to accept it while also being able to spot hot to tip negotiations into a positive direction.

For a deal in Czechoslovakia, for instance, I ended up bartering blue jeans in order to get some much-needed information from a local government official. I had been getting nowhere with him, and then happened to mention that I had a spare pair of blue jeans in my suitcase back at my hotel. I further noted that I thought they might be of his size. The doors suddenly opened and I received the required information and documents. This kind of thing happened all the time. In those days, if you wanted to do diplomacy behind the Iron Curtain, you had to bring extra pairs of blue jeans!

In the twilight years of the Cold War, when a divided Berlin stood as the living embodiment of global political tensions, I often found myself in a race against time that no financial spreadsheet could have prepared me for. As Nordic Bank's associate director in charge of, amongst others, the Eastern Bloc countries, I had become quite comfortable with the surreal

routine of crossing from the capitalist paradise of West Berlin into the grey communist landscape of East Berlin. Checkpoint Charlie had become my personal revolving door between ideologies as I conducted meetings with the Bank for Foreign Trade, all while relishing the return to creature comforts each night back in West Berlin.

Life was proceeding according to plan until March 1981 when I received an urgent message. A Finnish client, negotiating the sale of a particle board mill (because nothing says "exciting business venture" quite like particle board), needed an emergency meeting at the Leipzig Trade Fair. The catch? The client refused to discuss matters over the phone. He was convinced that East German officials were eavesdropping on their riveting discussions about wood products.

Thus began what could have been described as "Mission: Possibly Questionable," a 190-kilometre drive through East Germany to the city of Leipzig. Though I had travelled in East Germany frequently, I had never driven around on my own, nor had I been outside the main cities. Armed with assurances that the motorway was "good" (a relative term in 1981 Eastern

Europe) and a visa with the flexibility of Soviet bureaucracy, I set off in my rented VW, a Western-made and very non-Trabant-looking vehicle for the town of Leipzig.

For those unfamiliar with the automotive marvel that was the Trabant, imagine a lawn mower engine wrapped in what appeared to be reinforced cardboard. These smoking, puttering symbols of communist engineering dominated East German roads, making my vehicle stand out like a peacock at a penguin convention.

When I drove through the border at East Berlin, I received my first ominous warning. I had to be back and out of East Germany by midnight like some banking Cinderella whose loan terms would expire at the stroke of twelve.

"No problem," I said, unaware of the comedy of errors that was about to unfold.

The journey to Leipzig passed without incident. I enjoyed the rare privilege of overtaking virtually every vehicle on the road. This was not too difficult when your competition consists entirely of two-stroke engines powered by what appeared to be watered-down lighter fluid. A particularly humorous moment occurred at a motorway service station where my car stood alone among a sea of Trabants. One can only imagine the envious stares and suspicious glances from locals mulling the nature of capitalism..

After successful meetings about the thrilling world of particle board (the Netflix series is surely forthcoming), I began my return journey back to the West Berlin border with what I thought was plenty of time to spare. But fate had other plans. A traffic jam—presumably caused by multiple Trabants simultaneously running out of momentum—delayed my progress.

As the minutes ticked by, my anxiety grew. Approaching the border five minutes past midnight, I faced the stern faces of East German border guards—individuals not known for their appreciation of tardiness or comedic timing. Visions of diplomatic incidents, awkward calls to the embassy, and headlines reading "BANKER DETAINED OVER PARTICLE BOARD MEETING" flashed before my eyes.

Thanks to my negotiation skills honed in endless financing deals and my own brand of "humour," I was eventually allowed to cross back into West Berlin, exhaling a breath held since about 10 minutes before midnight.

Thus ended my first and only visit to the city of Leipzig.

Humour aside, it wasn't all cloak-and-dagger negotiations nor denim diplomacy. I witnessed firsthand the human cost of the Cold War divide. I remember several poignant moments in East Berlin, watching families on either side of the Berlin Wall waving to each other across no-man's land. Unlike so many of my countrymen in England and friends in all of Western Europe, I saw clearly what the political divisions were doing to families. They were torn apart and were not able to hug each other for years and years. Sometimes, this reality that I witnessed first-hand made all my business negotiations for investment projects seem quite trivial.

Despite the challenges and the often surreal nature of the work, there was a certain thrill in navigating such uncharted waters. Each successful deal, each visa stamp in my passport, felt like a small victory in the larger Cold War chess game. I felt like I was part of something bigger than myself and bigger than any of the projects that I was working on. I wasn't just doing business. I was both constructing bridges, buildings and factories, and also creating connections where none had existed before. That was a good feeling. As the 1980s wore on and the cracks in the Iron Curtain began to show, I found myself at the forefront of a changing world. Markets that had been closed for decades were beginning to open up. It was like a gold rush, but instead of

miners with picks and shovels, there were bankers with briefcases. I was a part of this opening up.

But I am getting a bit ahead of myself. It's true that I was very much building up a tool kit to capitalise on future developments of Eastern Europe. The Berlin Wall would still stand for another decade, but I was getting ready. But in the meantime, I would get yet another opportunity to do something that no one had done before, this time in yet another part of the world. I was faced with yet another offer to which I could not say no. After the Leningrad hotel project was put to bed in July 1979, Cyrus Eaton Jr. pulled me aside.

"I'm very happy with what you've done for me on this project," he said, a twinkle in his eye. "Would you be interested in a project in China? I've just come back from there."

My heart skipped a beat. China! The Sleeping Giant! Mao had died three years earlier in 1976 at the age of 82. Zhou Enlai had died the same year at the age of 77. Things were starting to change. After decades of turmoil, China had begun to wake up to the idea of international trade, and in 1979 after a couple of exceptionally turbulent decades, it was on the brink of a significant transition.

"Of course I'd be interested in a project in China," I replied without hesitation,

"Well, have I got a deal for you," Eaton said with a grin.

5

The Dragon's Dance

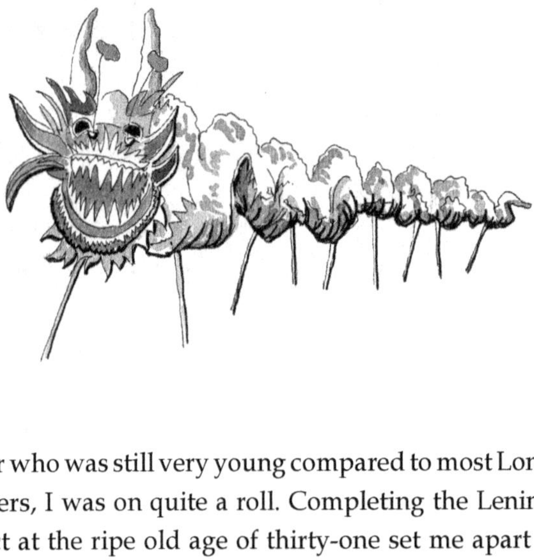

For a banker who was still very young compared to most London-based bankers, I was on quite a roll. Completing the Leningrad hotel project at the ripe old age of thirty-one set me apart from most of my peers. The many other assignments I completed in other countries behind the Iron Curtain as well in Asia along the way were simply the icing on top of the cake. I wasn't quite rock star status, but I was getting noticed by my bosses at Nordic Bank. I also had a new-found sense of self-confidence and even bullishness about what I could do. I was ready for anything.

For this reason, when the American industrialist Cyrus Eaton Jr. pulled me aside after the signing ceremony for the Leningrad hotel project to ask if I would be interested in a hotel project in China, it was quite natural and very easy to say yes.

I was hugely curious about the country. I had already spent a lot of time in Hong Kong so I had some understanding of the business potential of China. But, like many Western businessmen at that time, I was also in the dark on many issues. It was simply too early to know too much about the country that everyone had been calling 'Red China' for the past few decades. After the kickstart of "Ping Pong Diplomacy" in 1971, China and the United States began their dance towards rapprochement. First, it was Henry Kissinger's "secret visit" to China in July 1971 to set up an official presidential visit. Then in February 1972, President Richard Nixon landed in the PRC. At the time, the US government still recognized the Republic of China (ROC) in Taiwan as the legitimate government of China.

When I had been in and out of Hong Kong in the late 1970s, China was still a very closed and mysterious place. The effects of the Cultural Revolution still dominated even after Chairman Mao Tse-tung died in 1976 , the year I joined Nordic Bank. The new guy gradually appearing as the new paramount leader, Deng Xiaoping, was still largely an unknown quantity. He had been purged at the start of the Cultural Revolution in 1966, then 'rehabilitated' in 1973 before being purged yet again in the midst of the factional fighting between hardliners led by Mao's wife and pragmatists who knew that Maoist isolation was not the answer. Mao died in September 1976, his widow and her colleagues was seized the following month, and a couple of years later in late 1978, Deng managed to beat out his opponents in the Communist Party and set China in a new course. Diplomatic relations between Beijing and Washington were established from January 1, 1979, and China invaded Vietnam soon after, a short war that emphasised how far behind China had fallen. But market reforms in a number of areas were quickly rolled out, including the first hints of foreign investment being welcomed. Deng made an official state visit to the United States during which he famously wore a big Stetson cowboy hat and waved to a rodeo crowd in Texas. It was the beginning of a new era in US-China relations.

In 1979, China was still a desperately poor country. Most people were farmers, or closely connected to agriculture, and mostly organised into agricultural communes that were only dismantled in the early 1980s. In the cities, people were attached to state work units (*danwei*) which provided everything a family needed, e.g., employment, housing, healthcare, education, etc. Productivity across the board was extremely low and food shortages were common in various areas of the country. From late 1978 to mid-1979, as Deng Xiaoping was taking power and initiating his many market reforms, a wall in central Beijing not far from the Forbidden City, dubbed Democracy Wall, attracted "big character posters" and dynamic discussion on politics and the future of China by students and others. There were few foreign visitors to Beijing, and most foreign business discussions were conducted at the bi-annual Canton Trade Fair in the southern city of Guangzhou. As with the Soviet Union and the hotel project in Leningrad, it was hard to imagine much of a demand for a luxury hotel in Beijing. Foreign diplomats and VIPs on official visits to China would generally stay in state-owned hotels like the Peking Hotel. These hotels were strategically located near important government offices. Luxury comfort was not a high priority for the government, but keeping an eye on hotel guests was.

As described by Eaton, the China hotel deal that I would be responsible for putting together was enormous. I also could use some other words to describe the project such as revolutionary, ground-breaking, audacious, or even 'just plain crazy.' The deal consisted of a 10-year financing package worth $72 million with a fixed interest rate of five percent. This was significantly lower than the market rate at the time and for a while, market rates rose to 20 percent during the construction phase of the hotel. The funds would be invested in a joint venture hotel project the likes of which had never before been seen in Communist China.

For this project, I had the same questions that I had for the Leningrad hotel months earlier. Who would be staying in this hotel? Who would finance and guarantee such a project? Who would drive the project on the Chinese side? What was their key interest in such a project? If there were any profits, could they be repatriated out of China? Once again, the questions were endless, and the answers were hard to come by. But my job was to to do precisely this. Find the answers and get the hotel financed and built. I knew that I would need every ounce of creativity and determination to pull it off.

After the meeting with Eaton Jr, I had a meeting with KGB, my boss, to talk through the China project. It took a while to convince him that I was serious and that this was a plausible

Democracy Wall in Peking in 1979 from our moving car

and doable deal. But once he was over his initial scepticism, we began planning for the impossible. Not only was it a potentially lucrative project, but it could also, assuming we pulled it off, open all kinds of doors into The Middle Kingdom. Deng Xiaoping, the Chinese leader who suddenly ascended to the position of paramount leader in late 1978 and launched a whole slew of market reforms, was famous for his comment on pragmatism, that *"It doesn't matter if a cat is black or white as long as it catches mice."* With the Maoist approach to running China apparently due for a major shift, it was possible we were in a position to be one of the first international banks through the door.

One day, my lawyer (John East) and KGB were sipping champagne in the First Class section of a British Airways plane sitting at a gate at London's Heathrow airport, due to soon depart from Tokyo. They were on their way to China to help me nail the construction of what would be the very first international-standard hotel in China. Suddenly, the flight stewards escorted them off the plane, and British Airways staff informed them that a certain individual in Hong Kong, whose name was Ken Atkinson (ME!), had some important news for them. The meeting in Beijing had been postponed and the two of them had been rebooked on a different flight to Hong Kong which was waiting for them at another gate. I had set up this entire change in schedule without the benefit of email or cell phones and also worked out how to get the luggage to them. There was just one hiccup. Their suits were in the luggage sitting in the hold of the plane heading for Tokyo, and they would surely need them for the meetings in Hong Kong and Beijing.

In several hours, my boss and our corporate lawyer would be arriving in Hong Kong with only the clothes on their backs. They needed suits! But I had a friend who could solve that problem — Sam The Tailor in Hong Kong's Burlington Arcade. I arranged an emergency tailoring session with Sam and within 24 hours, I had two business partners with perfectly fitted suits and shirts in what was surely the most British response to a potential dress crisis. John and KGB's luggage arrived in Hong Kong a couple days later, so we were well prepared for our trip to China from Hong Kong, traveling in true 1970s style. This meant taking the train to Guangzhou and then catching a domestic Chinese flight to Beijing. With the help of Ms. Clara, we were able to secure "unbookable" First Class seats that were usually reserved for senior Communist Party leaders, but which could mysteriously become available for purchase when needed by the right people making the right contacts. The art of *guanxi* was alive and well.

The cherry on top of this Cold War-era caper was sharing First Class cabin space with a man KGB immediately recognised as "Cats Eyes Cunningham." He was a British World War II fighter pilot hero turned aviation consultant who was assisting the Chinese government with getting their newly designed aircraft airborne.

This delightful confluence of tailoring emergencies, diplomatic travel arrangements, and a chance encounter with a war hero perfectly encapsulated the Wild West feel of the early Western business forays into China. We had no idea if we were going to be able to pull the hotel project off, but at least we had new suits on.

So with a mixture of trepidation and excitement, we set off for China from Hong Kong, with a train from the border to Guangzhou and then by air to Beijing. The unexpected started the moment we arrived at Peking Airport, which was a tiny place dating from the 1950s. The baggage was moved from the plane to the terminal building on a trolley pushed by hand and then loaded onto a table in a small baggage hall. We then had to wait a full week for our first meeting.

While we waited, the three of us, my boss KGB, our go-to lawyer John East, and I, were treated to a whirlwind tour of Beijing's most important tourist sites. This ranged from the Great Wall to the Forbidden City and on to countless temples around the city, including the Temple of Heaven. The weather was close to freezing and all the locals were dressed in down-lined versions of the ubiquitous Mao suits with flaps strategically placed so they could relieve themselves without dropping their pants while squatting over a trough behind a privacy door about 6 inches high.

We also visited Mao's Mausoleum, where the former leader was interred under glass. But one of the most interesting trips was to parts of the Underground City, the tunnels which extended under the entire city of Beijing. It was built in preparation for a possible attack by the Soviet Union. The section we visited was on three levels with access through sliding floors in shops and other buildings. There was everything in the tunnels, including schools, hospitals and shops. It was essentially a bomb shelter that could house up to 300,000 people.

Every evening for the entire week, we were treated either to a banquet or escorted to one of the Beijing restaurants reserved for VIPs and foreigners. The presentation of the food was magnificent although some of the parts of different animals that were served to us were not so appealing to the Western palate. Banquets, of course, also required us to drink Mao Tai, the sorghum based spirit, which in my view based on extensive experience tastes like a cross between kerosene and nail polish remover. The goal was to get the foreigners drunk.

On my first several trips to Beijing, not wishing to upset my hosts, I ate and drank everything I was offered. I particularly loved the Big Duck Restaurant, several stories high on the far side of Tiananmen Square with the meal consisting of seven

Beijing street in 1979 behind the Forbidden City

or eight courses of duck. All the restaurants closed early. If you wanted to eat after 8 PM, the only choice was the "After Hours" restaurant in the Peking Hotel. Back then, there wasn't much nightlife, except for a disco with fairy lights at the Minzu (Nationalities) Hotel on a Saturday evening and seating space in the long marble-lined lobby of the Peking Hotel, dubbed by some as the "Street of Broken Dreams".

One of my enduring memories from that first visit were the convoys of trucks that came into the city at night and dumped piles of cabbages at different locations along the streets. They were covered up with tarpaulins and just left there with no security. Over the next day or two, these piles of cabbages moved from these pop-up sales centres to the balconies of the apartment blocks and stored for the upcoming winter months.

Eventually, we secured our first meeting with the China International Travel Service (CITS), a state-owned company which was to be the local partner for the project. We were first provided with an hour-long presentation about CITS and the project, with very little mention of any financial terms. It was as if they expected us to simply leave a suitcase full of cash at the door.

As we left that first meeting, my lawyer John East whispered to me, "I've never come so far to contribute so little."

"When you send the bill, just remember that you just had a free holiday in China," I whispered back.

While we didn't get much done on the hotel project on that first trip, it was a fantastic opportunity to be one of the first westerners to visit Peking after so many years of isolation. We visited all the major sites and had the opportunity to learn a little of the culture and the history of the country.

Undeterred by this inauspicious start, as soon as I returned to London I began drafting an information memorandum on the project, as well as instructing our lawyers to draft a loan agreement and accompanying documents that would be reviewed by a host of lawyers, bankers, and partners. The key challenge at hand was to syndicate a loan for a China project without any government guarantee for a term of 10 years and with a fixed interest rate of 5 percent. This was a monumental and unprecedented task.

After a lot of discussion and strategising, KGB and I identified the most important element to the project, which was that we needed to get the Bank of China to join the syndicate of lenders, even if it was just as a symbolic gesture. If their name was on the documents, it would appease other lenders and show them that we had official backing within China for the project. We also identified the person at the Bank of China who could make this happen, the well-respected Number Two at the Bank of China's London branch, KC Wu. KC had been in London before the Communist takeover in China in 1949, and had not returned. He was well known and highly respected in the City of London. Over a carefully orchestrated and sumptuous Chinese lunch in the private dining rooms of the Bank of China, we presented our proposal to KC and to his superior, Mr. Jin Dejin who was on secondment from the Bank of China's head office in Beijing. We made our pitch for the project and stated clearly that the Bank of China's participation in the syndication was needed to attract other lenders.

Our pitch worked. Within hours of the lunch, we received a phone call from KC Wu to say that the Bank of China was "in." This was the linchpin we needed. With this in place, the syndication came together relatively quickly. We also came up with a way to bridge the problem of the low interest rate. We negotiated with Eaton and his partners for an interest make-up arrangement to bridge the gap between five percent and Libor (London Interbank Offered Rate) plus a margin of profit. The main challenge was the period of construction of the hotel when there would be no cash flow. We agreed upon a US$5 million security deposit, which could be drawn against on a six-month basis to cover the interest differential. So in the end, the deal came together well, but the negotiations for the loan agreement took significantly longer largely because of the hosts' unfamiliarity with banking terminology and translation issues. I did what any banker would do to resolve such problems — I got on a lot of planes and had a lot of meetings to explain, pitch, explain some more, re-explain again, and do whatever it took to get signatures for the deal.

In the very early 1980s, traveling to Beijing from outside of China was quite an adventure. There were basically two options: fly in from Tokyo on Japan Airlines or fly into Hong Kong, take a train to Guangzhou, and then fly from there on a domestic flight. That was it. For international air travellers, there were just those two routes to the capital of China. Even with just these two routes, there were always surprises. On one flight that started in Guangzhou, the pilot announced that they were diverting the plane to Shanghai because... *it was dinner time!* The passengers, including myself, were puzzled, but since we were in First Class, we were shuttled into a fancy dining room reserved for foreigners and VIPs and treated to an exceptional meal. That certainly made up for the diversion. On the bus ride back to the plane, I found myself standing next to an American gentleman. Curious, I asked him who he worked for.

"General Motors," he replied.

I couldn't believe it! I told him that I only knew one person who worked for General Motors and that was my Uncle Len who had recently been transferred from Detroit to San Francisco.

"Do you mean Len Jackson?" he asked with widened eyes.

My jaw dropped. "Yes, do you know him?"

He did indeed, and he had just spent the weekend with my uncle before heading to China. There you go. Another "small world" moment and this time on a bus to an airplane after a flight diversion for dinner!

I made several trips from London to Beijing through both the available routes, constantly explaining the benefits that an international hotel would bring to China. I worked long nights with translators to get all the documents correctly translated into Chinese. This was only part of the challenge because for quite a few pieces of standard banking terminology, like LIBOR, profit before and after tax, audited accounts, commitment fees, margins and so on, there did not exist an agreed translation in the Chinese language as used on the Mainland, isolated for so many years from the international main stream. There was also no real understanding of many of these concepts among the finance team from CITS. However, I built up a good relationship with Li Wei, the leader of the CITS negotiating team, and we established a strong bond of trust by patiently explaining to each other the different challenges that we faced representing our sides of the deal. This worked well. One lesson that I have learned well from my time in China and elsewhere is to always put yourself in the position of the other side, because one-sided deals are almost guaranteed to fail.

I also considered myself to be quick thinking and tried to always keep my wits about me. For this hotel project, I was particularly proud of the insertion of a specific clause in the joint venture contract that stated that both parties were "jointly and severally liable" for the debts of the joint venture. This seemingly innocuous phrase effectively provided the guarantee of repayment from CITS. This made lenders more comfortable and the insertion of the phrase meant there was no need for an explicit guarantee from the government of China, which would have been far more difficult if not completely impossible to obtain. I worried that I might have taken advantage of my relationship with Li Wei, even though I spent a lot of time explaining the meaning of the clause to him, but in the end it worked out fine.

As the deal was coming together, I found myself constantly flying around the world. In fact, in a move reminiscent of Jules Verne, I circumnavigated the world in seven days in July 1980 to collect signatures on the final loan agreement and ancillary documents from banks and borrowers in London, Singapore, Hong Kong, Beijing, San Francisco, and New York. It was a whirlwind journey, among the first of its kind, and showcased the rapidly shrinking world of international finance facilitated by two flights on the Concorde.

With the documents signed and the project underway, the real work began. The groundbreaking ceremony at the hotel site in northeast Beijing took place in late 1980. Rather than this marking the end of the banker's role, it was just the start for me of a long and often tedious process of mediating between the American and Chinese partners. Every time an issue arose, CITS always required my presence as the banker and provider of the funds. I shuttled between London, Hong Kong, and Beijing nearly 100 times over the course of the project. This was from 1979 to late 1983 and beyond. I became the living embodiment of the growing ties between East and West.

As my trips grew in number and as time progressed, more and more foreigners started to appear in Beijing looking to do business. Over time, we had a small community of expats and the British Embassy decided to open their staff bar, The Bell, on Embassy grounds to Brits and friends of Brits. This meant I had a place to visit when I was alone. I formed friendships with people that still exist today such as Andy Andreasen, one of the first American students to come to China to study Chinese at the Foreign Languages Institute in Peking. Another was Frank Hawke, a fluent Mandarin speaker who was working for CB Sung, one of the foreign investors in the project. They helped with the translations and in particular the loan documents and other related documents. We spent hours and hours together and forged long lasting friendships, which continue today. Some of the other characters at the time were Mike Langley of HSBC who opened the bank's representative office in the Jianguo Hotel, the first joint venture hotel to open in China in 1982. What an oasis that place was. It was built using the same design plans as the Palo Alto Holiday Inn in California and had all the modern conveniences. This, of course, included a great watering hole called Charlie's Bar which rose to immediate fame (and fortune). Other expats at the time who I regularly socialised with and who helped me keep my sanity were Owen Nee from Coudert Brothers and Kerry Jelbart from National Australia Bank, one of the banks in the loan syndicate. A shout out to all you pioneers.

As the Great Wall Hotel project progressed from being a hole in the ground that in banking circles was at one point known as "Ken's folly," to a physical building, my reputation grew. Of course, as with any large construction project, there were delays in the construction. For example, there was one that involved an argument about the use of a new cement batch plant and cement trucks imported by the foreign side. When construction started, the concrete was mixed by the workers as the Chinese have always mixed concrete, which was by hand using small mixers. The finished concrete was then lifted up into the building in wheel barrows using ropes and pulleys. There were also delays caused by disputes over the quality of the curing of the cement and the fact that people were discovered sleeping on site in the depths of winter.

There were various rumours about the hotel that had to be constantly debunked as the hotel neared completion. To this day, I still hear the one about the rooftop restaurant that was originally supposed to be a revolving restaurant, but could not revolve as the revolving tracks had been mistakenly buried in concrete. In fact, the restaurant had never been designed to revolve. So goes the Chinese rumour mill.

CB Sung investor and Minister Chen Muhua

There is one story worth sharing that exemplifies the banquet and drinking culture that often prevails when Chinese officials host foreigners. It was during the Lunar New Year celebrations in 1981 and construction was underway on both the Great Wall Hotel and the Jianguo hotel closer to the centre of the city. CITS hosted a banquet for the representatives of both hotels and there were close to 20 tables. It was customary for people from the host table, at which I was seated, to visit every other table to offer a toast. Carrying our glasses of Mao Tai, we set off on our tour around the banquet hall followed by waitresses who were quick to re-fill our glasses after every toast. We completed our rounds and I asked my interpreter, who I had noticed kept putting matchsticks in his pocket after every table, what he was doing. He shared that he wanted to see how many shots I could drink. The meal continued and, of course, in true Chinese fashion all the other tables then wanted to toast each table one by one including the head table. I should say *especially the head table.* By the end of the evening, I was naturally a bit wobbly on my feet. My interpreter told me that I had drunk 33 shots because he had 33 matchsticks in his pocket to prove it. Apparently, it was a record at the time for a Caucasian. After that banquet, my nickname amongst the Chinese was Mr. San Shi San Bei (Mr. 33 cups). This was the equivalent of a full bottle of Mao Tai. I managed to get back to the Peking Hotel where I usually stayed in that era, but I had to stop to steady myself against one of the huge Dragon Pots in the lobby. I then fell asleep and had to be woken up by a couple of good-hearted foreigners who helped me to my room. In the morning, as I entered the breakfast room a person approached me and asked to take my pulse, which I could not understand for a minute. It turned out he was one of the two who had helped me to my room, and he had had a bet with his friend that I would not be alive the next morning.

During the construction phase, I was often onsite and observed day to day activities as the project came to fruition. The grand opening of the hotel took place in June 1984. It was a lavish affair with many high-ranking government officials and a large contingent of Americans including the US Ambassador to China. In the evening, all the key people peeled off to one of the various restaurants in the hotel, and then reconvened at the night club, which was truly a ground-breaking establishment for Beijing. For most of the Chinese guests, it was something they had never seen or experienced and they were awestruck.

Due to the success of the Great Wall Hotel project, I became known as a bridge between the Western financial world and the awakening Chinese market. I could navigate cultural differences and find innovative solutions to complex problems, which made me a valuable asset in the rapidly evolving landscape of China's links to international finance. I'm a lucky guy.

Beijing's Great Wall Hotel was not just any hotel, it was the first of its kind for China. It would soon be hosting a visit by US President Ronald Reagan, but only after a full and complete inspection by, among many others, myself as the banker. Picture the scene: A pristine ballroom capable of hosting 1,000 people, complete with one of modern China's first escalators (1930s Shanghai aside) leading up from the ground floor to the ballroom entrance on the first floor. Carpet layers were brought in from New Zealand to meticulously fit the expensive woollen carpet rather than the usual ceramic tiles. Everything seemed to be going well until I saw what can only be described as a very enthusiastic group of trainee staff ascending the escalator.

Now, in 1980s Beijing as well as other parts of Asia, spitting in public was as common as bicycles. Even the prestigious Peking Hotel maintained spittoons in its corridors, treating them like prestigious *feng shui* accessories. However, one eager trainee

The Great Wall Hotel under construction in 1982/3

decided to forego the traditional spittoon route and instead attempted to demonstrate his impressive trajectory skills while ascending this rare escalator, probably the only one in Beijing at the time. The projectile narrowly missed a New Zealand carpet layer and landed in the fresh carpet's plush embrace.

The next day, the hotel's joint venture chairman asked me to report on my hotel inspection and whether I thought it was suitable for foreign heads of state. Ever the diplomat, I praised the hotel's progress, but gently suggested that perhaps some staff habits might need a slight adjustment. I then shared what I had seen on the way to the ballroom the previous afternoon. One of the challenges was that the hotel had to offer employment to all people of working age who had been living on the site, most of whom were farmers.

Thirty minutes later, I was asked to return to the ballroom where, arranged like a Communist-era choir, were five or six rows of 30 to 40 staff members lined up police style. I was asked to walk up and down the lines and identify the expectorator.

In a moment of quick thinking that now sounds rather corny, I delivered what might be the most politically incorrect get-out-of-jail-free card, "I'm sorry, but I don't recognize anybody. They all look the same to me." That surely saved some poor trainee from some awful fate, and I am sure he appreciated by diplomatic declaration of ignorance. The Great Wall Hotel would go on to host President Reagan and countless other dignitaries, with significantly improved staff etiquette and cleaner carpets.

I became quite good friends with the hotel's first general manager. His name was Peter Sun (Sun Bai Da) and he was a nephew of Madam Soong Ching Ling, the widow of Sun Yat-sen, often referred to as the father of modern China. He knew I did not sleep early, mainly because of jet lag, and that I liked drinking in the evening. So he arranged to have a name tag placed on the back of one of the bar stools with instructions to the staff that if I were sitting in that seat, which was reserved for me when I was in residence, the bar should remain open. It was a great idea and I was very happy with it, and honoured to have my own stool. However, neither Peter nor I imagined that one early morning the staff would call him at 4 AM to ask if they could ask me to go to bed so they could close the bar. I got the hint and called it a night.

I also remember the opening of the Kiss Club in the hotel in 1984. This was one of the earliest and most iconic night spots at the time, with the exception of Maggie's bar. The music was Western and good to dance to, but as you looked around at the staff, they were often standing perfectly still and upright as if they were totally oblivious to the beat of the music. They really didn't know what to do. This was just a reminder of both how far the city had come and how far behind many of the residents of the city still were. Of course, it's all a far cry from today.

The banquets continued as did the dinners in the local

restaurants. Some of the local restaurants were actually quite good and worth visiting. One of my favourites was the Big Duck on one of the corners of Tiananmen Square just behind Mao's Mausoleum. It had seven or eight floors of tables and always appeared to be very busy. The other duck restaurant we used to frequent was the Sick Duck, so named because of its proximity to one of the local hospitals.

The financing story of the Great Wall Hotel wasn't just about numbers and contracts. It was about building relationships and trust across what had for decades been vast cultural divides. My friendship with KC Wu and interactions with figures like Chen Muhua, the Minister of Foreign Economic Affairs, highlighted the human element that underpinned these groundbreaking financial deals. These relationships were crucial. Our London lunch with KC Wu helped to secure the deal, but more importantly it implied a guarantee from the People's Republic of China. It was an indication, especially for me, that sometimes a nod from the right person can be worth more than any written contract. I had learned how that was done, and my expertise in Chinese financing led to a string of new opportunities, including a consulting contract with Nordic Bank after I left my full-time position there to run my own consultancy. My reputation as a "*Lao Pengyou*," an old friend of China, would follow me throughout my career. This opened doors and created opportunities that others could only dream about. I had about a 10-year head start on everyone else because of my success with the Great Wall Hotel project.

One such opportunity came in 1987 when I decided to purchase an apartment in Hong Kong. I reached out to my old acquaintance from the Bank of China London branch, Mr. Jin Dejin, who had become the head of the newly established Ka Wah Bank part of CITIC. I found myself treated not as a client, but as a trusted friend. The ease with which I was able to secure a mortgage and the discovery later that no lien had been placed on the property, spoke volumes about the trust and respect I had earned in Chinese financial circles.

This trust, however, came with its own set of challenges and responsibilities. As I navigated the complex world of Sino-Western business relations, I often found myself walking a tightrope between different cultural expectations and business practices. The rapid changes in China's economy created both opportunities and pitfalls, as demonstrated by my experience with the Hong Kong property market. I decided to sell the apartment after it doubled in value. This seemed prudent at the time, but in retrospect, it showed how even the most experienced players can underestimate the explosive growth potential of the Chinese market.

The challenges were numerous. Language barriers, differing business cultures, and the ever-present spectre of political uncertainty made every deal a complex dance of diplomacy and finance. As the 1980s progressed and China's economic reforms gathered pace, I found himself at the forefront of a financial revolution. The skills and connections that I had built during the Great Wall Hotel project positioned me as a key player in the burgeoning market for Chinese investments. Western companies, eager to tap into the world's most populous market, sought my advice and expertise. Chinese officials, recognizing my understanding of their country and its needs, welcomed me as a trusted advisor. I was a regular speaker at events promoting China as an investment destination.

But success in this new frontier came with its own set of ethical dilemmas. As I brokered deals and facilitated investments, I was acutely aware of the potential for exploitation on both sides. I strove to ensure that the projects I worked on were not only

The Great Wall

profitable but also beneficial to China's development. This commitment to ethical business practices sometimes put me at odds with more aggressive investors, but it also earned me the respect of my Chinese partners. This latter group was arguably more important.

Just a few months after closing the Great Wall Hotel deal, I received a summons from my managing director. With a mixture of curiosity and trepidation, I made my way to the executive suite. The managing director's face was a mask of confusion and concern.

"Ken," he began. "We're getting these enormous deposits from the Bank of China. Can you explain why?"

My mind raced. The bank only had capital of 10 million GBP. Why and from where was this flood of money coming? Then, it dawned on me. This was reciprocity, Chinese style.

"I think it has something to do with Chinese culture," I explained. "We signed a loan agreement to lend them $72 million, and now they are depositing $72 million with us. It's their way of building trust and showing good faith."

The managing director's eyebrows shot up. "Mind-blowing," he muttered.

This incident was my first taste of the complexities of doing business in China. It was a world where relationships, or "*guanxi*," were paramount, where trust was built through grand gestures, and where the lines between business and friendship were often blurred.

As I delved deeper into the world of Chinese finance, I found myself rubbing shoulders with some of the most influential figures in the country's economic transformation. One such figure was Rong Yiren, the head of the China International Trust and Investment Corporation, a man who later became a Vice Premier of China, and his colleague Jing Shuping, the head of China International Economic Consultancy (CIEC).

In the days before the communist victory in 1949, Rong had been a successful businessman in Shanghai and he and Jing were rising stars in the new Chinese world of Deng Xiaoping. Rong seemed to take a shine to me and often picked me up in his Cadillac for lunch at exclusive restaurants, such as Maxim's, when I was in Beijing. "Call me anytime you're in town," Rong said to me, extending an invitation that would make most Western businessmen salivate with envy.

But I hesitated to do so. I was young, naïve, and not too sure how to take full advantage of such an opportunity. I didn't want to waste his time and didn't think that I had a lot to offer him. I felt this way even though Nordic Bank was the first foreign lender to make a loan to China International Trust and Investment Corporation (CITIC) Bank a loan of $20 million. Knowing what I know now, I would probably have behaved very differently back then.

This reluctance to fully leverage my connections was both

a blessing and a curse. On one hand, it allowed me to build genuine friendships and earn a reputation for integrity. On the other hand, it may have limited my ability to capitalise on the immense opportunities that were unfolding in China. And they were most definitely unfolding. As my reputation grew, so, too, did my network of contacts. I was brokering a range of deals and facilitating relationships between Chinese institutions and Western banks. The $20 million CITIC loan facility was a crowning achievement for Nordic Bank. The deal was revolutionary at the time and cemented the bank's relationship with CITIC and CIEC and perhaps more importantly two key individuals, Rong and Jing.

To celebrate the CITIC deal, I assisted in organising a visit for the Chinese delegation to London. I still have photographs from this trip. To me, they capture a moment of cultural exchange and budding friendship that I believe helped to shape the future of Sino-Western economic relations.

One of my most cherished relationships was with Jing, the

With Rong Yiren (and interpreter) and Jan Ankercrona in Nordic bank in 1983

head of China International Economic Consultants. He was a man of depth and complexity, a survivor of the Cultural Revolution who had seen his books, including his beloved Bible, burned by the Red Guards.

I learned about this on the visit and asked a Nordic Bank secretary to go to St. Paul's Cathedral in London to purchase a leather-bound Bible with gold-edged pages. On the group's last evening in London, I presented him with this gift. The usually composed Chinese official was overcome with emotion, tears welling in his eyes. From that moment on, I had a friend for life. Years later, I was recovering from cancer surgery in a Hong Kong hospital when an aide of Rong and Jing arrived with a case of bird's nest soup, a traditional Chinese remedy believed to have healing powers. To this day, I have no idea how he even knew I was in the hospital, much less that I was recovering from cancer surgery.

The various stories of the Nordic Bank deals in China and my

With Jing Shuping outside the Tower of London in 1993

involvement with projects such as the Great Wall Hotel project and the CITIC loan (although this was not my direct deal), became pretty well known within banking circles. I developed a good reputation that I believe was well earned. Because of this, when I left Nordic Bank to build my own consultancy, I had a lot of work lined up. In fact, Nordic Bank initially became my most important client. My journey through China led to work in many other countries, but the greatest value I gained from my China experiences was a clear understanding of the importance of personal relationships how they are, and have to be, intertwined with business interests. A small gift, such as the Bible that I gave to Jing or the bird's nest soup that I received from him, could move mountains when a project was in its early stages. At the end of the day, there is enormous value in looking past the balance sheets and profit margins and focusing instead on the human elements that underpin all business dealings. In the world of international finance, cultural understanding and appreciation is just as valuable as, and perhaps even more than, financial acumen.

Flying Behind the Great Wall

"I can't fly on CAAC with them because the flight is sold out," I told the Chinese Ambassador to the United Kingdom.

The Ambassador had asked me if I was flying back to Beijing with Rong Yiren and Jing Shuping, two high officials who were returning to China after the Chinese delegation's tour of London, which I had helped to arrange. The trip was part of the financial deal for CITIC in Beijing.

"Don't worry," said the Ambassador. "I'll see what I can do."

Of course, within the hour, the Chinese Embassy called to say, "We've got you a seat."

I really, really didn't want to fly China Airways (CAAC). Before they got their new Boeing aircraft, we jokingly, dark humour here, said CAAC stood for China Airline Always cancels. I didn't want to go, but I took it in stride. But in terms of politics, politeness and logistics, I really had no choice. I was heading back to Hong Kong anyway and it was a stopover to China. However, the aircraft that awaited me on the tarmac looked like it had been around the block a few times and maybe should have been in the airplane graveyard. The "First Class" cabin resembled a Siberian gulag with wings, complete with arctic temperatures and flight attendants who appeared to have graduated from the charm school of the damned. When I dared to request a blanket to combat the cold, the attendant looked at me as if I'd asked for a private performance of the entire Beijing Opera.

The only bright spot came during a refuelling stop in Bahrain. All the passengers, including Rong Yiren and his entourage including me, by now resembling well-dressed popsicles, were ushered into a palatial VIP room. The buffet spread before us might as well have been a mirage after the horrors of the flight. My fellow travellers and I attacked the food with the enthusiasm of people who had just crossed the Gobi Desert on foot.

But this flight was merely the appetizer for my buffet of aeronautical misadventures in China. On one domestic flight within China, I witnessed something straight out of a Marx Brothers movie. As the plane began taxiing, I spotted a man running alongside the aircraft banging on the fuselage with a stick. In any other country, this might have triggered a security alert. In China, it simply meant that they'd forgotten a passenger. The pilot, displaying a remarkably casual attitude toward schedules, simply stopped the plane. The door was opened, and the windswept passenger was shoved aboard. My fellow travellers barely batted an eye at this impromptu game of catch-the-plane, treating it as just another Tuesday in Chinese aviation.

The crown jewel of my flying follies occurred on a flight from Xi'an to Beijing. Shortly after takeoff, the captain made an announcement in Mandarin that sent the Chinese passengers into concerned muttering. My own grasp of Mandarin was limited to the basics of "hello," "thank you," and "where's the toilet?" so I turned to my seatmate to see if I could learn anything more.

"Minor problem with propeller," he said. "We go back to airport."

What followed was a comedy of errors that would have given any Western aviation inspector a heart attack. The plane landed with a thud that suggested we had made it back to runway.. Mechanics swarmed the engine. Their approach to aircraft maintenance can best be described as "hit it and hope." After twenty minutes of percussion-based engineering, they gave a thumbs up.

This cycle repeated itself three more times. Take off, fly for a bit, turn around, land, watch men hit things with hammers, and then take off again. By the fourth attempt, I was seriously considering making a run for it, but where would I go? Being stuck in Xi'an was no joke, and I had to get back to Beijing.

The mechanics, now consulting what looked suspiciously like "Aircraft Repair for Dummies" finally got it right on the fourth try.

When we landed in Beijing, I was ready to kiss the ground, much to the amusement of my fellow passengers who seemed to view the whole experience as nothing more extraordinary than a slightly bumpy bus ride.

One of my final misadventures in early China aviation took place on a flight from Dalian, a city known for its glassware. I nearly missed this flight due to an unexpected roadblock. There was a dead horse right in the middle of the street that was blocking all traffic. By the time tractors had removed the equine obstruction and I reached the airport, it was well past check-in time. But in the topsy-turvy world of Chinese air travel at that time, schedules were more suggestions than rules. The flight had been held for me. It's not clear if they knew about the dead horse.

The cabin resembled the aftermath of a glassware convention. Boxes of delicate glasses from the Dalian factory occupied most of the seats and none were secured in any meaningful way. Myself and two other passengers were squeezed in amongst this fragile cargo, feeling like human bubble wrap. As the boxes shifted ominously during take-off, I imagined the potential incident report: "Passenger lost in freak glassware accident. Last seen somewhere over Manchuria."

Years later, I look back on these adventures with a mix of horror and fondness. They were part of a unique moment in history when the world was divided not just by ideology, but by wildly different approaches to air safety. I would tell younger colleagues, "You haven't really traveled until you've flown Aeroflot or Chinese airlines and lived to tell the tale." They would laugh, thinking I was exaggerating for the sake of effect. If anything, I was understating the case.

As air travel has become increasingly standardized and globalized, I sometimes find myself missing the wild unpredictability of those early days. Sure, modern air travel is safer, more comfortable, and far less likely to involve impromptu engineering sessions in mid-flight, but it also lacks a certain charm and sense of adventure. There is no thought given to the possibility of one day having to run down the tarmac, suitcase in hand, chasing after a departing flight.

My adventures in early Chinese (CAAC) airspace taught me valuable lessons about patience, adaptability, and the importance of always packing a good sense of humour along with my passport and an extra pair of Y-fronts. They had also given me a lifetime's worth of stories to tell, each one a little window into a world that, for better or worse, no longer exists.

So the next time you find yourself grumbling about a delayed flight or a cramped seat, spare a thought for myself and my compatriots who braved the skies of the Eastern Bloc and China all those years ago. Remember that somewhere out there, there's probably still a mechanic with a hammer, ready to solve any aviation problem with a good whack and a prayer. And be thankful that, these days, that mechanic is probably not working on your plane.

6

The Hong Kong Hustle

Hong Kong. As a Brit, the name of this quite small island just off the southern coast of China had a nice ring to it. Up to the Handover in 1997, it was "our island," one of the last physical remnants of the British Empire. Of course, we still had, and have to this day, the British Commonwealth, but Hong Kong was different. It was a colony of Great Britain. British citizens had full rights to live and work in Hong Kong, and many young people of my generation did exactly that. Some worked in hotels or bars, some using the enclave as a home base and traveled around the region. Still others launched business ventures with Hong Kong as the commercial hub. Whatever the reason, the colony beckoned and welcomed people like me.

I have never been an historian, but I found the story of Hong Kong fascinating when I was working there. This was before the age of faxes, computers, and emails, and my 'historical point of view' came more from the James Clavell novels *Taipan* and *Nobel*

House than any history book. That said, I would like to share a bit of the history of the territory that was my home for more than a decade.

In 1839, the first Opium War broke out although it should have been called the Tea War. The English had become addicted to tea over the previous century, and the only source of the tea leaves was China. But China was ruled by the Manchus, and they wanted nothing to do with the English or any other foreigners, and would only take silver in return for the tea shipments. This caused a silver shortage and slow-burning global financial crisis and the British had to find a commodity the Chinese market would accept to balance out the tea trade. They found it in opium. The British had recently taken control of most of India, where the best opium was grown, far better quality and cheaper than Chinese domestically produced opium, and so the British, including such traders as William Jardine and James Matheson, started smuggling it in and buying tea leaves (and porcelain vases and silk) in return. The Manchu's Qing government objected, and the Opium War commenced, and it was no contest. The Qing military were no match for the British naval forces, and as part of the surrender agreement in 1842, the British took control of Hong kong island and the harbour to its north as a colony in perpetuity, while also opening up a number so-called treaty ports along the China coast, including Shanghai.

After the second Opium War, Britain gained the Kowloon Peninsula and Stonecutter's Island under the Convention of Peking in 1860, and a few decades later in 1898, Britain secured a 99-year lease on what was named the New Territories which was adjacent to Kowloon as well as some surrounding islands. The lease agreement was set to expire in 1997, which set the stage for Hong Kong's eventual return to China.

Due to its strategic location in East Asia, Hong Kong was

an ideal base for British trade with China, Southeast Asia, and beyond, and while it was overshadowed by Shanghai, it was an important hub for trade between China and the West. During World War II, from 1941 to 1945, it was occupied by Japan, but after the war, Hong Kong was returned to British control and the government immediately began rebuilding. In the 1950s and 1960s, with China closed and an influx of refugees and most importantly Shanghai business people after 1949, Hong Kong's economy transformed itself into a manufacturing hub. In the 1970s, Hong Kong's manufacturing base, which had been churning out cheap textiles, garments and plastic toys for markets around the world, began to shift towards financial services. The city emerged as one of the world's leading financial centres, with a dynamic economy driven by trade, banking, and a burgeoning stock market. It became one of the "Four Asian Tigers" that experienced rapid economic growth during the latter half of the 20th century.

Throughout all these growth years in the 1970s and '80s, everyone knew that the business life of Hong Kong had an expiration date. If the signed treaties were adhered to, the New Territories would revert to the control of the People's Republic of China in 1997, and no one knew with any degree of confidence what might come next. As this date approached, Britain and China began negotiating Hong Kong's future. These efforts culminated in the Sino-British Joint Declaration in 1984, in which Britain agreed to hand over the entire territory to China in 1997. In return, China promised that Hong Kong would enjoy a "high degree of autonomy" for 50 years under the "One Country, Two Systems" framework. The handover officially took place on July 1, 1997. On that day, Hong Kong was officially "handed back" to China which ended more than 150 years of British colonial rule. Under the new arrangement, Hong Kong became a Special

Administrative Region (SAR) of the People's Republic of China.

By the time 1997 rolled around, there had been several developments that impacted on the agreement which been signed in 1984. There was the eruptions across China in 1989, while in Europe, the Berlin Wall fell and within just a few years, the Soviet Union had disintegrated and the Eastern European countries had been largely transformed.

When I was living in and doing business from Hong Kong in the late 1970s and 1980s, the island colony was a fascinating mix of East and West. Its legal system was based on British common law, and it had an independent judiciary. The political system, shaped by the colonial administration, became somewhat more participatory with the establishment of the Legislative Council even though universal suffrage was not fully implemented. English was the official language, along with Cantonese, and traditional Chinese culture remained a strong influence on daily life.

Of course, Hong Kong today in 2025 is a very different place from what it was in the 1980s and in the first decade after the Handover in 1997. The birth of Hong Kong, as the modern city it is today, came through its colonisation by Britain, and because of the Opium Wars, a group of islands that only had some small fishing villages on them became one of the world's most important financial centres. Today, it is ever more integrated into the economy of China.

Before the Great Wall Hotel project in Beijing, I had already been in and out of Hong Kong numerous times. It was not yet my home base, but it was getting close to being so. I still had a London-based job with Nordic Bank even though I was constantly on the road and was rarely physically in London. Asia beckoned and, because of my experience and growing network due to the successful Great Wall Hotel project in Beijing, China was the focus. There were deals to be done and I felt that I needed to be there on a more full-time basis. The strategic decision of choosing Beijing, Shanghai, or Hong Kong as a base for business operations in Greater Asia was hardly a contest. Hands down, Hong Kong was the logical choice.

For 150 years, the biggest and most influential trading houses of Asia, the likes of Jardine Matheson, Swire, HSBC, and others, had been registered in Hong Kong and done business there. They had built up an infrastructure for doing business around the world. This was obvious to me. But there was something else too. I loved the energy, the street food, the restaurants and the noise, and the trams and public bus services, which made life so convenient along with the relatively inexpensive taxis. In its own way, Hong Kong became my home.

The Chinese market was opening up and I found myself in the enviable position of being one of the few Westerners who had successfully navigated the treacherous business waters of China. There were very few people who had done deals there

The Forbidden City in Beijing

and even fewer who had done deals that also made money. I was in a rare position of having accomplished both. If China was a newly discovered gold mine, I was in the business of selling mining equipment as well as helping people find and tap the country's most lucrative veins of gold.

Back home in London, I actually had it made. I had earned a reputation for identifying problems and then solving them. At a moment's notice, I was more than capable of jumping onto planes to fight financial fires on behalf of Nordic Bank in locations all over the globe. I also had two quite impressive deals on my resume, the Pulkovskya Hotel in Leningrad and the Great Wall Hotel in Beijing. With just those two deals alone, I could have probably demanded a big office with a cushy job and a lucrative career at Nordic Bank.

But I didn't. Asia beckoned. Hong Kong was calling. However, I needed a nudge to help me jump off the ledge and dive into the ocean of entrepreneurs. In this ocean, there were no big corporate home offices to save me if I started to drown. There were also a lot of sharks. The rewards were high, but so too, were the risks.

The life of a jet setting businessman might have appeared glamorous but it made family life a difficult thing to maintain – it was situation many others found themselves in in those years. But it turned out okay in the end and my two kids turned out great in spite of, or who knows, because of my absence, although I always maintained close contacts either through monthly visits to UK or their spending school holidays in Hong Kong with me.. Life moves on for us all but the important thing is we still have a close relationship.

My first nudge came from Winston Ko, an American Chinese businessman, for whom we had arranged financing for the Golden Flower Hotel, the first-ever foreign invested hotel in the city of Xi'an in the northwest of the country. He offered me a 50-50 joint venture, which he would fund and I would assist him on his deals on a discounted success fee basis. We had a few successes, the first one being the shipping of a mothballed hand tool factory from Chicago to Beijing. The factory was the contribution of the foreign partners to a joint venture with a Chinese state-owned company. The fee Winston negotiated made my jaw drop. It was double what I ever imagined we could get, but he researched the background and knew the factory had been fully written off. Our joint venture worked well until 1986 when he wanted to develop a new computer system and the costs of a London office and a Hong Kong office were starting to take their toll. So, we negotiated a separation agreement. The second and final tipping point came from a Swedish hotel chain that had had its eyes on me for some time, because I had introduced them to their first hotel management opportunity in Asia, that is the Golden Flower Hotel in Xi'an. The hotel management company was owned by the Swedish government which, if needed, could add a pretty substantial safety net to any of its projects. They were ready to make an offer for my services once the separation with my American Chinese partner was complete. I dealt with the partnership issue, but then I had to see to my own needs and negotiate a contract to replace the joint venture which was, in fact, an already well-established partnership that offered consultancy services with offices in Hong Kong and London. The role with the Swedes would not be limited to Asia. It would also cover Europe and North America. In the end, it came down to a pretty basic question.

How much should I charge these guys?

It was 1986. The more advanced economies of the world were recovering from a deep recession, while developing countries struggled with debt and stagnation. In Asia, Japan had become the second largest economy in the world and the four

Meeting Chris Patten at the Hong Kong IOD

Tiger Economies of Asia (Hong Kong, Singapore, Taiwan, and South Korea) were just beginning their rapid industrialisation transformation as they moved from being low-income backwaters to lower-middle and then upper-middle middle-income powerhouses. High-income status was at least a decade away for them, but they were on their way to that status. China, on the other hand, was in the very early stages of its transition to a market economy. It was still poor, and it attracted the most attention only because it was so enormous.

My pitch to the Swedish company had four key components. First, I wanted a guaranteed eighty days of work per year, spread over all four quarters of the year. Second, I wanted a significant daily rate. Third, I wanted the contract to be London-based. Fourth, I wanted them to pay all my travel costs between London and Hong Kong including hotel stays. In addition, I would be allowed to use their Hong Kong office as my home base when I was on the job for them. I was asking for the moon, but I had seen how Swedish executives did business in Asia and other parts of the world. They would burn money with stretch limos at JFK Airport in New York City, a whiskey bar in the limo, hotel suites (not rooms) in the best hotels, and for dinner they would order lobsters the size of small dogs.

Still, it was a gutsy move. For three nail-biting weeks, I waited for their response with my stomach doing somersaults worthy of an Olympic gymnast. To my surprise and delight, they agreed to all my terms. With the prospects of making some pretty serious money, I decided to continue with offices in London and Hong Kong, and I never worked less than twenty days per quarter on their projects. For a start-up entrepreneur, I could not have asked for more. I had one very solid client, life was good, the money from their fees was enough to sustain my then standard of living plus a little, and I was free to work for other clients in the time they were not utilizing my services. I was doing well.

Among all the quintessential Chinese traits that I had to learn about in order to succeed at business in Asia and in particular in China, *feng shui* probably tops the list. The word *feng* means 'wind' and the word *shui* means 'water.' *Feng Shui* is a philosophical system that is basically as old as China itself. It focuses on harmonising people with their environment. For the Chinese, wind and water, i.e., *feng* and *shui*, are elements that are vital for life and are connected to good health and prosperity. The key principles of *feng shui* included many things such as:

1. **Qi** (chi) which is the vital life force that flows through everything including people.
2. **Yin and Yang** which focuses on the balance of passive/active, dark/bright, and feminine/masculine.
3. **The Five Elements** which are wood, fire, earth, metal, and water. Each of these elements are associated with certain qualities and, of course, they must be balanced.

4. **Bagua** is like a *feng shui* energy map that is used to organise spaces according to the flow of qi.
5. **Orientation and Placement** which is the strategic placement of all kinds of objects from a work desk, furniture, doors (especially the front door of a home or business), windows, entire buildings, and even how cities are planned and laid out.

The Chinese were extremely serious about *feng shui.* It dominated so many aspects of family and business life both in China and Hong Kong. For the Chinese, it had to be done right or the consequences could be catastrophic. A current and highly visible example of *feng shui* in practice involves the China Central Television (CCTV) building in Beijing. It was completed in 2012 and took more than a decade to plan and build. It's a large, 51-story building with two towers joined at the top with a cantilevered extra slab of offices extending out into space and back again. The whole thing is known locally as "Big Pants" and it features a 36-metre high hole in the middle. The leading architects for the building were from the Netherlands, and the goal was to create something unique and striking, and by golly they succeeded. There are those who say the hole is meant allow the wind to pass through to meet China traditional *fengshui* requirements, and I choose to believe that is the case.

Of course, I didn't know any of this in the beginning when I set up my own shop in Hong Kong.

In fact, I messed up right off the bat. One day, early in my Hong Kong career, I went for a client meeting at their premises. It was early on in our negotiations, and I didn't yet have any kind of agreement or contract with them. When I arrived at their office, I was ushered into a meeting room, and started looking around, picking up various ornaments to look at more carefully. I

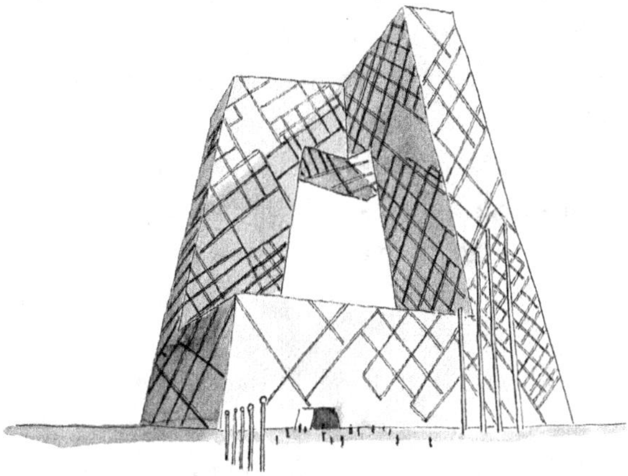

Sketch of the CCTV Building in Beijing

would then place them back where I had found them. I also noticed a painting on the wall that was crooked so, helpfully I thought, I re-aligned it. I was basically waiting for the meeting to begin and I have never been too good at just sitting still. I was also very curious about all the artistic items that I saw in their office. But when the meeting began, we discussed nothing. Every time I tried to introduce a tangible point about the pending project, my potential involvement, detailed questions that I needed answers to, and so on, there was silence or just some generalities battered about. I could tell something was wrong, but I didn't know what it was.

Later on, I realised my poking around, picking up items, and straightening a crooked picture frame had done a lot of damage. I had messed with their *feng shui*. My prospective client had no interest in talking about the normal business issues of balance sheets, margins, investment, the potential project, and so on. They were far more worried about how I had altered their office's *feng shui*. More than anything, they wanted to get me out of the office so everything could be put back into balance. After this one episode, I sometimes used this a tactic when I was not ready to discuss or negotiate a deal.

In terms of work, my newly found consultancy practice had turned me into a financial Sherlock Holmes. I had learned quite a bit about this kind of work when I was with Nordic Bank. One case that stands out was in 1978. It was the reason for my heading back to Hong Kong after my return from the Singapore month secondment. I was charged with checking and confirming some extravagant spending and questionable business practices of the person who was employed as the managing director. The director lived in a lavish town house on Strawberry Hill on the Peak, one of the most expensive areas in Hong Kong. The rent for the house was $2,500 per month, which in those days was enough to buy a small island in the New Territories. He also felt he deserved two luxury cars, a Jaguar and a Ford Granada, even though a company car had been assigned to him. When told to get rid of the Jaguar, he sold it to a leasing company and then had it leased it back to the company. He would also leave the safe in his office open because he could never remember the combination and also had a habit of leaving the office early. In addition, he usually left the office door open even at night when he left for the day. When the cleaners arrived to do their job, they would lock the office after leaving.

In some ways, I was the "executioner" and had to make tough calls based on people's behaviour. As best I could, I took on this job with a sense of duty and I hope a bit of humour. However, this commitment to integrity sometimes came at a personal cost. In one case, I had to act on behalf of a provisional liquidator appointed by the High Court of the British Virgin Islands. It was to oversee the management of a business during a shareholder dispute. One of the directors on the losing side, who despite being a long-term resident of Ho Chi Minh City, has never spoken to me since.

The environment of Hong Kong in the 1970s and 1980s was a bit like what I imagined the old American West to have been with gunslingers and sheriffs. Business malpractices were common and I was like a sheriff doing what I could to protect the people who hired me. It was a game of financial whack-a-mole but I became pretty good at wielding the mallet.

It all came at a cost, but I was making really good money at the start of my Hong Kong consultancy. And life in Hong Kong was great. I was making more money than I had been making with my joint venture and by base revenue was essentially guaranteed. My timing for this China advisory and business development role had been perfect. But despite my financial success, I never fully embraced the "Yuppie" lifestyle that was prevalent in the 1980s. For example, rather than leasing or buying a Jaguar and Granada like the guy I had investigated had done, I preferred to take taxis or public transport. Hong Kong's nightlife was vibrant and I would hang out at places like Mad Dogs, Joe Bananas, the Godown, and the nascent Lan Kwai Fong. I hated just sitting around my hotel room or my leased apartment or eating on my own. Instead, I would go to bars and restaurants and just start chatting with people. After a few drinks, we would inevitably get a table and continue our conversations over dinner. These impromptu dinner conversations often led to new friendships and business connections. It was networking Hong Kong style over a bowl of wonton noodles, some pub grub, or whatever was available, while we talked about business, family, friends or just shared commiserations about Hong Kong's humidity.

Amid the fun and games and the need to understand important cultural cues like *feng shui*, Hong Kong taught me a very important and fundamental lesson about the value of integrity. At times, even with the establishment of the Independent

Commission Against Corruption (ICAC), it seemed that all of Hong Kong still operated in shades of grey. The ethical shortcuts were numerous and common. Within this kind of environment, I had to find something to rely on and I focused on doing what I thought was "the right thing", even when it came at a personal cost or loss of some short-term profits for myself or my clients.

As the 1980s progressed, my consulting business flourished. I was at the forefront of China's economic opening. I had a unique blend of Western financial expertise and hard-earned understanding of Eastern business practices. This made me an invaluable asset to companies looking to tap into the burgeoning Chinese market. Boastfully, I could say that I was the financial equivalent of a Rosetta Stone, translating the languages of Western capitalism, Eastern *guanxi*, and mindfulness of cultural traits like *feng shui*. I had also come to a realisation that, in the world of international finance, success is about more than just crunching numbers or making deals. It's about understanding people,

With Laura and Robert at Joe Bananas in Hong Kong

navigating cultural differences, and maintaining one's ethical compass even when it might be easier to look the other way. It's also about a re-definition of the bottom line. Not everything is about profits. It's also about the stories, the relationships, and the occasional misplaced artistic ornament that can derail a multi-million-dollar deal.

At one point, my frequent flyer miles to China almost turned me into Her Majesty's most financially responsible secret agent. The year was 1986. Margaret Thatcher was in power, the Cold War was still giving everyone the chills, and I was racking up more trips to China than your average ping pong champion. While I thought I was merely plying my trade in the Middle Kingdom, someone in Britain's intelligence community had apparently decided that anyone making that many trips to China must be up to something more exciting than explaining depreciation methods or putting syndicated loans together.

One day, while I was in Beijing arguing about decimal points over dim sum, a mysterious brown envelope arrived at my office in the Barbican. Now, in the world of spy movies, brown envelopes usually contain top-secret documents or mysterious microfilms. In this case, it contained something far more terrifying: a letter from Great Britain's Ministry of Defence asking for a chat.

Upon my return, like any good citizen, I dutifully called the number. This led to a meeting that could only have been scripted by someone who had watched too many spy movies. Enter stage left, a man wearing a bowler hat and carrying an umbrella, looking about as inconspicuous as a panda at a polar bear convention.

As if reading from a playbook, this walking stereotype proceeded to question me about my Chinese contacts with all the subtlety of a foghorn in a library. I had no idea what he was going on about, and it wasn't until I mentioned the encounter afterwards to a friend of my father, a former Scotland Yard man, that the penny finally dropped. They were trying to recruit me as a spy!

Just imagine the possibilities. International Banker turned 007 Spy. My weapon of choice? A particularly sharp pencil. My gadgets? A calculator that also shoots lasers (but only after proper depreciation). My catchphrase? "The numbers are stirred, not shaken." My cover could have been perfect. After all, who would suspect a banker of being a spy?

But being the sensible chap that I was, I realised that acting as a double agent might put a slight damper on my budding business relationships. It's generally considered poor form to spy on your clients, especially when you're trying to build a reputation as a trustworthy financial advisor. When Mr. Bowler Hat came back for a third meeting, I had to let him down gently. No license to kill for me. Just a license to continue practicing my business skills, thank you very much.

I later had a much more amusing brush with "espionage." Fast forward to 1997, Julie and I moved to Ho Chi Minh City and took up residence in what I used to describe as a wedding cake house in the alleyways of D1 in Saigon.

In these alleyways, I discovered that real espionage isn't conducted by men in bowler hats or through brown envelopes. No, the real masters of intelligence gathering were far more mundane and far more effective: the taxi drivers of Ho Chi Minh City.

One day, I visited my regular money changer to exchange a $100 bill. Later that same day, Julie tried to make her own currency exchange, but her taxi driver dropped an intelligence bomb that would make MI6 blush with envy, "Madame, you don't need to change money. Your husband changed $100 this morning."

While British Intelligence was still fumbling with bowler hats and mysterious envelopes, the taxi drivers of Ho Chi Minh City had perfected their own intelligence network. The weren't just transportation providers; they were an interconnected web of information gatherers, sharing intelligence with the efficiency of a Silicon Valley startup and the accuracy of a Swiss watch. The irony wasn't lost on me. Having politely declined a career in British Intelligence, I found himself under surveillance by the one of most efficient intelligence networks I had ever encountered.

What is the moral of this tale? Perhaps it's that the best spies aren't the ones in fancy cars with ejector seats who look like the actor Daniel Craig. They are those who know your daily schedule better than you do. Or maybe it's that when it comes to intelligence gathering, nothing beats a well-organised group of taxi drivers with good communication skills.

As my China career grew throughout the 1980s, I was also drawn to new countries and regions within Asia. The combination of the Fall of the Berlin Wall and Tiananmen in 1989 had an enormous impact on global business. And despite my rich experience, I began to understand that, by the end of the 1980s, my 'China Experience' had mostly run its course. As a small consultancy, I could not really compete with the major firms, who could invest enormous human and financial resources in a project. Simply put, China had become too big and I had remained a small consultancy. I simply could not manage all the relationships that needed to be managed for a project of substantial size in China. I was beginning to think of other options.

And so it was that on June 1, 1989, I signed a contract to conduct a feasibility study for SAS International Hotels for a hotel project in Hanoi. Three days later, I watched along with millions of people around the world as army tanks rolled into Tiananmen Square in Beijing to crush a student rebellion. Though I still had investment projects in China up through the late 1980s, I was coming to the conclusion that I needed to be in other markets to survive. Tiananmen impacted China-Western relations for a considerable time and many businesses and business consultancies suffered a dramatic fall in activity and revenue. I, however, had my eyes set on a new market in Asia. I was going to Vietnam.

7

EARLY *DOI MOI*

The first inkling that I might be destined for a long-term career in Vietnam occurred on June 4, 1989 in Bangkok. Specifically, it was during my morning coffee when I opened up the *Bangkok Post* newspaper and read, like millions of others around the world, about the tanks rolling into Tiananmen Square in Beijing. I was precisely three days into a consulting contract for a new hotel project in Hanoi. On June 1, 1989, I had signed a contract with Scandinavian Airline Systems (SAS) International Hotels to conduct a feasibility study for a new international hotel project in Vietnam's capital city. Like with any new project, there were no guarantees that it would work, but at least I had a contract. I would be going to Vietnam for the very first time, to begin work on the feasibility study.

I had a lot to learn about the country. I had never been there and the extent of my knowledge, like a lot of foreigners, was mixed in with Vietnam's wartime history. I needed a crash course in Vietnam's post-war history, and so that's what I did. I learned a lot.

On the morning of April 30, 1975, the war in Vietnam was over. General Duong Van Minh, the last president of the Republic of South Vietnam, who had been supported by the United States for most of his country's existence, had surrendered. He ordered all the troops under his command to lay down their arms. After decades of war with the French, the Japanese, the French again, and finally the Americans, peace had arrived. Ironically President Minh's number 2 became one of my best auditing service clients, for a prestigious hotel he was building in the centre of Saigon. In April 2025, Vietnam celebrated the 50th anniversary of the re-unification of north and south as Liberation Day. I was happy to be in Saigon and to be part of that celebration.

On July 2, 1976, the Socialist Republic of Vietnam was officially established and its leaders set out to recover from decades of war and destruction. In its Second Five Year Plan (1976 to 1980), the new government proposed some extremely ambitious plans including annual GDP growth of 15 percent, industrial growth of 17 percent, and agricultural growth of 10 percent. Of course, none of these goals were met. Instead, there was triple digit inflation, the currency was changed twice with very little forewarning, and there was very little economic activity. Vietnam had to import food and fuel to survive. In the first several years after unification, one of its primary exports was scrap metal, the debris of many years of war. Beginning in 1978, Vietnam engaged in a 10-year long guerilla war with the Khmer Rouge in Cambodia. Also beginning in 1975, tens of thousands of Vietnamese tried to flee Vietnam by boat. This was the beginning of the Boat People Crisis. Untold thousands died in the attempt. Others managed to survive their ordeals by sea to arrive in refugee camps and eventual re-settlement in numerous countries around the world, in particular the United States, France, and Australia. The attempts to leave Vietnam by boat lasted for about 10 years. In the late 1980s, there were many Vietnamese who found themselves "stuck" in Hong Kong refugee camps with no countries willing to sponsor them. After languishing in these refugee camps for years, many of them ultimately decided to return home to Vietnam. They had no choice but to try and re-start their lives. Before my move to Vietnam, I had a couple of friends in Hong Kong who were working in the refugee camps and a couple of them are still in Saigon today.

Vietnam's post-war policy mishaps are too numerous to detail in this memoir. The very succinct description of Vietnam from 1975 to 1986 is that the country was extremely poor and barely surviving. There was little sense of hope among its citizens. They were looking for something new and a man named Nguyen Van Linh, a member of the Vietnamese Communist Party's ruling Politburo, had some new ideas. Beginning around 1983, Linh wrote and published a series of articles in the state media about the numerous problems that Vietnam was going through and the need for reform. When he became the Party's General Secretary in 1986, he pitched these ideas to the 6th Party Congress. For many Vietnamese, they were the first glimmers of hope after a decade of despair.

General Secretary Linh's policy ideas are called '*Doi Moi*' which translates into English as 'New Change' or 'Renovation.' When the policy shift first became known on an international level, it was sometimes referred to as 'the perestroika of Vietnam' even though the beginnings of *Doi Moi* (e.g., the Nguyen Van Linh articles in 1983) preceded Mikhail Gorbachev's reform movement in the Soviet Union by several years. The initial goals of *Doi Moi* were relatively basic. Among other changes, *Doi Moi* put into place a trend of decentralization of decision-making from the central government to the provinces. This empowered provincial government leaders to begin to plan for the financial future of their regions. There was a liberalisation of agriculture, moving from, commune-style farming to farmers having more control over their fields and what they produced, as well as the right to sell on the open market. The state would no longer provide price supports or subsidies. In addition, Vietnamese were now allowed to found and own businesses and, more importantly at the time, manage the plot of land assigned to them. A new land law proposed the "radical idea" of giving farmers various usage rights, including the transfer and exchange of land usage to others, the right to bequest to their heirs, or rent out or mortgage their plots as they wished.

Like with any new policy, the changes were incremental from the late 1980s through to the mid-1990s. Vietnam was and is still controlled by a single party, the Communist Party of Vietnam. The economy was still mostly state-controlled even if some private sector activity was being allowed. There were family-owned enterprises for trading and retail businesses, but there were virtually no small to medium-sized private companies in other sectors of the economy. State-owned enterprises (SOEs) had the most land, had access to bank loans, and were mostly protected by the state from outside competition. In some senses, they couldn't fail because the state would always step in to provide a subsidy or roll-over an overdue loan despite the SOE's inherent weaknesses. There were some hints of a market economy emerging, but the state involved itself in so many aspects of the business economy that entrepreneurial ideas could not take root nor get financing if the idea did manage to take root.

I saw many of the same people I had seen in China in the early 1980s now beating a path to Vietnam, but most of them soon left with their tails between their legs. Vietnam was not the same as China in spite of the many similarities. In the early 1990s, the Vietnamese were still feeling their way along the reform path. This was the same for the Chinese in the early 1980s, but Vietnam had no significant foreign exchange reserves such as China had accumulated from their trading through the Canton Fair years before they opened their doors to investment.

Despite the promise of *Doi Moi*, this was the status quo of the late 1980s. It is feasible that this status quo in Vietnam (i.e., state control, limited free market activity, a limited role for the private sector, and restraints to a full market economy) would have remained intact for many years and even decades if not for some politically disruptive events on the other side of the world. In the city of East Berlin, Germans were also ready to try something new.

After months of protests on the streets of East Berlin and with thousands of East Germans fleeing into Austria through an open border gate in Hungary, the Berlin Wall collapsed. Thousands of East Germans flooded into West Berlin and West Germany. Within just a few days, there was no longer a barrier between east and west Berlin, and the country of Germany was reunited. Since end of World War Two, the world had been roughly separated by the United States view of the world and the Soviet Union's view of the world. Most countries had to choose and side with one system/country or the other. This ended with the fall of the Berlin Wall in 1989. Within a year or two, the rest of Eastern Europe, the countries behind the Iron Curtain, were radically changed and the Soviet Union transitioned from being one very large and powerful entity into 15 separate countries.

The Soviet Union had helped to keep Vietnam afloat during

the war years with America and after the war ended in April 1975. It provided soft loans, technology, barter trade, and the opportunity for many Vietnamese to study and work in Eastern Europe. They earned foreign currency which greatly helped their families back home. After the breakup of the Soviet Union, Vietnam no longer had ideological friends in Eastern Europe nor a benefactor that could help it along financially. Within just a few months in 1989 and 1990, the world as Vietnam knew it and the world as it knew itself no longer existed and Vietnam had to figure out how to move forward. The new policies called '*Doi Moi*', then three years old, was a good starting point. But more to the point, these policies *had* to work . There were no backup plans for Vietnam and its economy. *Doi Moi* was the one and only path.

In some ways, my timing could not have been riskier. When I signed the consulting contract on June 1, 1989 (just three days before the army tanks rolled into Tiananmen and a few months before the Fall of the Berlin Wall), the political and economic future of Vietnam was totally up in the air. The *Doi Moi* policies were still vague concepts rather than tangible laws and policies.

When I first arrived, in November 1989, the Foreign Investment Law had been promulgated months earlier and apart from the Civil Code there was not much else in the way of laws and regulations. At the time, Sweden was helping Vietnam develop its tax laws. The country's most important benefactor, the Soviet Union, was in the process of collapsing and was barely able to feed itself. There were other stress points as well. After the war ended in April 1975, the United States had imposed and strictly enforced a full trade embargo on Vietnam. This had numerous crippling impacts. For example, many multi-lateral institutions could not work in the country nor lend it money. Many large privately-owned companies could not sell products and technology to Vietnam due to the risk of running afoul of the US Embargo. The European company Airbus, for example, could not sell aircraft to Vietnam because their planes contained American-made parts. Of course, Boeing could not sell anything to Vietnam.

When I arrived in Leningrad in 1979 to build a hotel, the Soviet system was still firmly in place. When I arrived in China that same year for another hotel project, the system was in a leadership transition, but there was some stability as well as a desire to transition to a market economy and embrace outside foreign-invested projects. In 1989 in Vietnam, there was political stability, but who could hazard a guess as to its financial future with so much of its previous support network in complete turmoil? Vietnam was still one of the poorest countries in the world. Average per capita income was less than US$100 and foreign trade added up to just US$5 billion a year and only a couple of FDI licenses had been issued. It was ostracized by the United States which would bully other countries to also ostracize and isolate Vietnam. There was not yet any kind of signal that the US government would relent and begin to engage with the country. Russia, one of the friends Vietnam still had from the Soviet Union days, was a friend, but not a stable or wealthy friend. The road to be travelled into the future by Vietnam was unclear and unknown. It had always been good in battle with "the other," whether the "other" was China, France or America, or indeed the Khmer Rouge in Cambodia. But by the end of 1989, there were no more "others" to deal with. Vietnam had to plot a new course forward, and the only policy framework it seemed to have in hand was a set of ideas called *Doi Moi*.

In such an environment, was advising on financing and building an international standard luxury hotel in Hanoi in 1989 the right choice for entrepreneurial consultant like myself? It was a big gamble. There was no tangible evidence or not even much of an indication of what Vietnam's next moves might be. What path would it choose? The examples provided by several Eastern European countries who were also trying to transition to a new system resulted in war and misery for many of them. Would Vietnam pursue the creation of a relatively free market, a foreign-investment friendly type of environment? Or, would it stick to develop a socialist-heavy, command economy structure with state-owned companies firmly in control? Or in a worst-case scenario, would the turmoil of the formerly communist countries of Eastern Europe be exported to Vietnam?

These were the choices in front of me, but I also had no choice since I had signed a contract. At a minimum, I had to get started. Of course, when I signed, I did not know the significance of what was to happen in Tiananmen Square and beyond on the night of June 3 and the morning of June 4, when the tanks rolled in. What started out as a student protest in mid-April (after the reform-minded Leader Hu Yaobang died) calling for reforms and a crackdown on corruption, turned deadly. In fact, we had visited the square a few days earlier and commented on the party-like atmosphere and the friendliness of the students. After that, the world for a time turned against China. Foreign investment deals all over the country dried up. I had a friend who was the general manager of the Golden Flower Hotel (my second project in China) in Xi'an that was quite popular before the 1989 troubles. After June 4, the hotel was virtually empty, and to keep the staff occupied, he started the hotel's own football team and a choir. They had football matches and concerts but mostly for the staff themselves. There were simply no guests, business people or tourists, staying at the hotel. My China deals were typically based on the assumption of success, and with no business activity, there could not be much success. It was hard to imagine a future for myself in China.

As noted earlier, I had already had what could best be described as '*a feeling*' that my China business life had almost run its course. I was relatively successful. I had made good money as a business consultant and helped my clients get many projects off the ground. I had endured a lot of hardship and frustration, made a lot of friends, and developed my *guanxi* well. But there were always ominous signs popping up here and there. Even in the early days of my own business in China, I had been warned about the difficulties. This was not so much about doing business in China, but about actually making money in China which, of course, is the point of doing business. I was making some money by helping others with the "doing business in China" part, but those businesses themselves didn't always make a lot of money.

One rather cryptic conversation I had with a Chinese colleague in around 1986 has always stuck with me. "Wei Jian Xin (my Chinese name)," he said, "it's great that you started up your own company in Hong Kong to do China work and that you want to continue working in China, but always remember at least one thing, which is that not even big companies make money here."

It was a frank and friendly caution from a key aide of Rong Yiren who had started up China International Economic Consultancy. This 'caution' came from a guy who had quite direct access to the top leaders of the country. He was someone in the know at a time when everyone in the world seemed to want to do business in China because of, among other things, its enormous market of one billion consumers. I definitely listened to him and trusted him, but just to be sure, I stuck around for five more years. I guess I can be a bit slow at times, but I usually get there in the end!

Come June of 1989 and with a contract in hand, I was about to

Ho Chi Minh Mausoleum in Hanoi in 1989

embark on something new. In more ways than I would have ever imagined at the beginning, Vietnam was a breath of fresh air.

As noted earlier, up to that point in time, the extent of my knowledge, and even the extent of my curiosity, was mostly about the war with America in the 1960s and '70s as well as the border war with China in 1979. I learned about that just as I was concluding my first visit to Beijing, as there was no foreign language news at that time. Nordic Bank had done a small trade financing deal for Vietnam in 1978, but this was completed entirely from London. It was a six-month trade finance operation that was paid off and closed without any issues. I didn't really work on the deal.

This time around, though, I definitely had a deal on my hands. It was a $20 million hotel project in Lenin Park in Hanoi. This was a very big foreign investment project for Vietnam at the time. The Great Wall Hotel in Beijing, by contrast, was around $72 million. Though I signed a contract on June 1, I didn't actually get to Vietnam until November that year. In the interim, I had to do a lot of re-organising work due to the collapse of so many deals in China. This included closing down my London office and extricating myself from a handful of China projects that were in various stages of development or disintegration. I did, however, continue to work on various projects in China through 1991.

For the Vietnam hotel project, the local partner was the Hanoi Tourism Services Company. They were the ones who got my visa sorted out, booked our hotel, and organised a car for the ride from the airport to Hanoi. In those days, the only entry apart from Moscow to Vietnam was through Bangkok. This is where we collected our visas and took one of the three flights per week to Ho Chi Minh City or one of the two flights per week to Hanoi. I remember that ride from the airport to the city so clearly. It was around 42 kilometres on what were entirely small one-way roads. We passed a lot of burned out military vehicles and old and abandoned gun turrets. Even though it had been 14 years since the American War had ended, there was still all this war debris along the road from the airport to the centre of Hanoi.

That first trip was a whirlwind tour of Vietnam. Together with a lawyer from Baker McKenzie Thailand and a business consultant from Thailand, we had a series of meetings over four days in Hanoi and three days in Ho Chi Minh City. I liked Vietnam pretty much right from the start. The people were really nice and very friendly. I sensed that they were very open to new ideas. The market was ripe with potential deals and there seemed to be a real acceptance of foreigners getting involved with projects. Of course, part of the reason was that we had, or at least the Vietnamese thought we had, access to investment capital. However, it was more than that. There was a genuine energy for making their own lives better. They wanted to make projects work and so they went the extra distance. This was quite different to the business environment in China where *guanxi* ruled and small firms like my own could only get so much done. In hindsight,

China was simply too big and complicated for a firm of my size. There were multiple locations that *guanxi* had to be deployed in order to be successful. If a company or a consultant like myself did not have enough the right connections at the right levels, it was hard to get anything going. Vietnam, by contrast, was less than one-tenth the size of China in terms of population and there were only two prime locations for doing business, Hanoi and Ho Chi Minh City. This was more manageable.

But maybe most of all and really much more important was the fact that I began to fall in love with the energy of the people and the place. Saigon, in particular, had great energy. It really was a city that never seemed to sleep. The city and its people just kept on going deep into the night. In China, I had been to countless dinners and banquets, and they were all interesting and memorable. The food was good, the drink was free-flowing (if you liked Mao Tai), and the conversations were fun. However, by 8 PM or so when the hosts had plied us with enough alcohol to ensure we slept soundly and we were tired of talking about business, we were escorted back to the hotel and the night was over.

The old American Embassy from the British Consulate on Le Duan Street in 1998

It was so different in Vietnam. After the food was consumed and we were all in a good mood from drinking with no intention of getting drunk, we piled into the host's cars or cyclos and went to a night club or a dance hall and kept the party going. This was more my style and it reminded me a lot of my early days in Hong Kong. I was also struck by the differences between Hanoi and Ho Chi Minh City. In the early 1990s, I had a conversation with an official from the State Committee for Cooperation and Investment (SCCI), the forerunner of the Ministry of Planning and Investment (MPI), who said that he did not want the two major cities of Vietnam to become just any other Asian cities. He and his colleagues wanted both Hanoi and Ho Chi Minh City to preserve their current charm. To me, after I got to know the place better, Hanoi and its citizens seemed more aligned with Europe. Over time and as I got to know more Vietnamese in and from Hanoi, this sentiment made sense because many Hanoi business and government leaders had studied in Eastern Europe and of course the strong French influence.. The SCCI official, who had also studied in Eastern Europe, wanted to do what he could for Hanoi so it would retain its character and I have to admit (I'm English), its French charm. To this day, I appreciate Hanoi's charm, the way it has taken care of the Old Quarter and the beauty of and opportunity to walk around Hoan Kien Lake which is right in the centre of the city. The idea of Saigon being a freewheeling Asian business capital and Hanoi being a more traditional European-style capitol city somehow spoke to me.

As for the hotel deal, it seemed quite promising. The project came my way from the first General Manager of the Golden Flower Hotel in Xi'an in China. He was by then in charge of business development for SAS International hotels (now known as the Radisson Group) who I was working with on a project in Beijing at the time. The hotel group's basic strategy was to set up international standard hotels in destinations that Scandinavian Airlines flew into. In the late 1980s, SAS was planning to extend its flights from Stockholm to Bangkok by adding a short leg to Hanoi, the capital of Vietnam. For this reason, the idea of building a hotel in Hanoi took shape and quickly moved from the idea stage to the feasibility stage. My job was to take a view on whether a profitable project could be put together with the backing of a consortium of Nordic banks and investors.

Of course, this was not so straightforward. The project was a $20 million joint venture to build and operate a 282-room hotel. The local partner was the Hanoi Tourism Services Company, which had been allocated the plot of land earmarked for the project, situated in Lenin Park. This was a very large public park which featured the Hanoi Circus and the most popular attraction, the burned-out shell of an American B-52 bomber which had been shot down during the 1972 Christmas bombing raid on Hanoi. City officials used the plane's carcass to promote local tourism and to commemorate the country's successful fight against the Americans. It was rumoured to have been shot down over Hoan Kiem Lake with Pete Peterson (the first post-war US Ambassador to Vietnam among the crew). Ironically and right from the start, a key stumbling block for the hotel project was the paucity of commercial financing options due to the US Embargo on Vietnam. The embargo prevented numerous businesses and banks (American-0owned or otherwise) from doing business with the country. It meant no major international bank could provide financing or any kind of loan guarantees to the project. It had to be done via multi-lateral institutions that were not constrained by the US Embargo.

So in addition to preparing financial feasibility forecasts on room rates, occupancy, returns on investment, and so on, I had to cobble together a group of institutions that would be both willing and able to participate in the project. This was from quasi-government funding agencies like Finnish Export Credit and its counterparts, Swedish Export Credit, Norwegian Export Credit and their aid equivalents. This took longer than a normal business loan, but it was also a bit less problematic. These organisations were created to handle projects such as this. The Swedish International Development Agency (SIDA), for example, helped to finance the Bai Bang Paper Company, one of the very first large foreign-financed projects in Vietnam.

I managed to get the financing agencies together and we had a deal on our hands, which by my calculations was quite attractive, revenue with very conservative revenue and financial forecasts. I assumed an average room rate of $80 per night and an average occupancy of 60 percent. The other hotel project in progress was the renovation of the Metropole Hotel which had originally opened in 1901. I stayed there for one night in 1990 before it closed, and it was not a great experience, but it was renovated and re-opened as the Sofitel Metropole in 1993, and it was charging over $200 per night and running at over 95 percent occupancy in its first year of operation. By my calculations, our hotel project would have earned its capital back in two and one-half years. We were all quite excited about it.

Signing documents for the SAS Hanoi Joint Venture in 1991

But, of course, real world politics (or maybe I should say 'Old World' politics) entered the picture. The foreign financing institutions requested that the foreign operator, meaning SAS International Hotels which had a very lucrative management contract to run the hotel, invest $2 million into the deal as operating capital. This would mean that they had some skin in the game. I did the calculations and decided the deal still worked, so I recommended to SAS that they should make the investment. Everyone agreed, but it could not get final board approval in Brussels and the deal was not approved. I assume there may have been some negativity arising from the American War (as it was known in Vietnam) or from the US Embargo. Whatever the cause, just like that, the deal began to crumble.

Of course, I had been around the block, and had seen such circumstances before. So fairly quickly and because of the inherent merits of project, I was able to help find a buyer in Singapore, a Swedish company which took over the project and paid me fees while I sought out other new partnerships.

From my perspective, the hotel deal was a success. I had put together a potentially profitable project, I was paid for my work, and I was able to salvage the deal, at least in the short term, by finding a new buyer when the original stakeholders backed out. Finally, I had proven to myself and to others that Vietnam was a place worth checking out, and that I was someone who could help to make things happen. In fact, the hotel project changed hands three times and for a variety of reasons ultimately never got off the ground. Yes, Vietnam was in its infancy as a market economy, and yes, its banking system had limited experience with the concept of commercial lending. Also, foreign banks and other large companies couldn't do business in Vietnam because of the US Embargo. Despite all those issues, I saw opportunities. I knew that the US Embargo would eventually get lifted, I knew that banks like the Bank for Investment and Development of Vietnam (BIDV) would gain a better understanding of commercial financing because, in part, I was working with some of their senior managers to help them understand syndicated loans and the international norms for loan agreements and agency agreements amongst banks. But probably most importantly, I had come to know the Vietnamese people and appreciated their energy, enthusiasm, and overall friendliness about getting business deals done for the betterment of themselves, their companies, and their country. For these and other reasons, I was intent on sticking around after the Hanoi hotel project.

By 1990, I had closed down my London office, and I was spending less and less time in Hong Kong and more and more in Vietnam with only a little bit of time invested in China. More than one year had passed since the Tiananmen "incident" and it was increasingly clear that business was not going to return to its pre-1989 state anytime soon. I also looked at Myanmar (Burma) which was an attractive option for a number of reasons. It was a former British colony (1886 to 1948) and much of its business economy and professional services were based on the British Companies Act. It was at that point opening for business and the country was quite rich in natural resources. It looked promising especially under the potential leadership of Aung Sun Suu Kyi whose political party, the National League for Democracy (NLD), started gaining momentum around 1988. In the presidential election of 1990, the NLD won by a landslide with Suu Kyi set to become the President of Myanmar. But the ruling junta refused to acknowledge the election result and placed Suu Kyi under house arrest.

So because of these two tragic global events (Tiananmen and the jailing of Aung Sun Suu Kyi), Vietnam became part of my destiny. The key challenge suddenly became how to found a privately owned consulting business in Vietnam with the goal of facilitating foreign investment. I wanted to help people "do business in Vietnam" but I also wanted to help them make money. In order to accomplish the "do business" part, I felt I should be based in the south of the country, but until 1993 when my first business license was granted, I spent most of my time in Hanoi, a city filled with so much charm. I rented a house in Thuy Khue Street with a rooftop view over the West Lake, and a private lawyer in Hanoi kindly allowed me to share his office. It turned out that he was the co-author of the Foreign Investment Law, and I still have the pleasure of working with that same firm today and I now work with the lawyer's son and granddaughter. In those days, there were two flights a day from Hanoi to Saigon, with both leaving at the crack of dawn using Tupolev planes, the only passenger aircraft that Vietnam had. A couple of these were involved in fatal accidents and some multinationals did not permit their staff to travel directly between Hanoi and Saigon, but required them instead to travel via Bangkok. My journey down Thuy Khuy Street to catch the early flight often involved witnessing the slaughter of a pig in the middle of the street. Not something I can say that I enjoyed.

Hanoi in those days had a very small expat community with only about six restaurants that we would frequently go to. My favourite was 202 Ba Trieu, famous for its crab farcie. It was started by a former driver from the French Embassy who spent his time, when not driving, helping out in the kitchen and learning the art of French cuisine. A more unique Vietnamese experience was provided by Piano Bar One and Piano Bar Two, two restaurants just around the corner from each other which were owned by the same family, but by different family members because they had apparently had a falling out.

There were some real characters in Hanoi in those early days, among them the pioneering lawyers Mark Lockwood and Tony Foster, who both now live in Saigon as does John Goodyear, the first "investment banker" in the group, together with Leigh Scott

A trip to Mai Chau in 1992

Kemmis. John is a neighbour in the residential complex in which we live.

All of these activities were well before Grant Thornton, and also before Bourne Griffiths. At the time, my situation was actually not much different from when I had set up my first business in Hong Kong nine years earlier to do work in China. The one difference was that this time, I had no financial backing. I was not working for a bank, nor did I have an anchor client guaranteeing me a set number of days of work per quarter. My goal was to set up a consulting business and bring foreign companies into Vietnam along the lines of how I had done it in China, except now I was completely self-employed. For 18 months, I was going back and forth between Hong Kong and Vietnam, and with the SAS hotel project, I experienced first-hand how the US Embargo was impacting business development. But I found a solution to that problem for the project, and I also firmly believed, as I stated earlier, that eventually the Americans would relent and lift the embargo. It was just a matter of time, and I wanted to have something tangible set up for when that eventuality occurred.

Long story short, I ended up with what's called a Business Cooperation Contract (BCC). This was one of the means for foreign companies to invest in Vietnam. Other ways included setting up a joint venture with a state-owned Vietnamese company, a Build-Operate-Transfer (BOT) project with the government (this was usually for infrastructure projects), and in some cases a 100 percent wholly-owned foreign company. This latter option was relatively rare in the early 1990s, but became more popular in the 2010s and beyond. For the BCC, a foreign company would sign a contract with an existing Vietnamese company or organisation to do business which set out what each side would contribute to the operation for a specific line of business over a specific period of time. In my case, it was business consulting, which was a new industry for Vietnam. It took some time to get the BCC license mainly because the Vietnamese authorities were wary about the deal since they had no experience in licensing a foreign consulting service company. During this time, from around 1990 to 1993, I was still commuting back and forth from Hong Kong and Vietnam.

First office in Ho Chi Minh City in 1993

I eventually signed a BCC with the Cho Lon Investment and Import-Export Company (Cholimex). Cholimex was active with import-export trading and some real estate, but its core business was food production. It was established in 1981 and was (surprise, surprise) founded by Chinese Vietnamese. Prior to 1975, Cholon was and had been for the previous 100 plus years the Chinese district of Saigon. Cholimex later became a household name for food production especially its range of sauces (chili sauce, soy sauce, oyster sauce, etc….)

We set up the PCS Cholimex Business Center in an office in District One of Ho Chi Minh City, just across the street from the Rex Hotel. For the first five years, we were directly upstairs from the ticketing office for Aeroflot Airlines. With my business license in hand, I moved to Ho Chi Minh city on a permanent basis in 1993. I was ready to help foreign companies "do business in Vietnam," and I was determined to help them make money as well.

Having said that, it was not only about making money for me personally along with my clients. It was also about being a pioneer and being the first to do something interesting in a new environment, country, and culture. I was an early bird for Vietnam. I got in on the ground floor earlier than most, and for this reason, I was frequently approached by newcomers asking for advice and seeking the benefit of my experience. This was generally done over a simple lunch or a drink (which often was the only compensation). I am happy to say that many of these people are still here, and we still meet regularly for dinner or for drinks at the Nag's Head.

***

The Reluctant Brawler

If anyone ever tells you that bankers and accountants lead boring lives, let me introduce you to my life. While being considered as a professional working in an industry where people wear suits and ties and are respectful of each other, I also managed to compile a collection of unexpected physical altercations that would make Jackie Chan proud. As it turns out, I can really take a punch or at least act like I can.

This history began in the 1960s at Sheffield University when I crossed paths with a group of rugby players inside one of my favourite watering holes, the Broom Hill Tavern or the "Tav" as it was commonly known. Now, if you're unfamiliar with rugby players, imagine human bulldozers who consider bruises to be fashion accessories. I was minding my own business and on my way home when I suddenly found himself surrounded by these gentleman scholars. What happened next is a bit fuzzy, but I was seeing more stars than the Hubble telescope and blood was gushing from my broken nose. That later led to breathing problems that made me sound a bit like Darth Vader trying to blow out birthday candles.

I was not new to clinches. My younger brother and I often wrestled and fought much to my mother's dismay. But, the real crown jewel of my "fighting career" came during what should have been a simple mini cab ride in London around 1993 with my companion Julie. We were on a trip over from Hong Kong, and the evening started innocently enough in Beaconsfield at my brother's house. But on the way back to our hotel, our driver apparently decided that the shortest distance between two points was through every back alley in Greater London. When I asked him why he was taking the scenic route through what appeared to be the setting for a Charles Dickens novel, the driver responded with all the grace of a wounded rhinoceros. He slammed on the brakes and demanded that we exit the vehicle. When we were out of the cab and in the street, the driver suddenly remembered he was owed money.

"Where's my 40 quid?" he demanded.

Channeling my inner legal eagle, I calmly explained the flaw in the driver's logic.

"I'm sorry, but you didn't take me to the place I had asked you to take me, and you threw me out of the cab. I'm not paying."

This application of contract law didn't sit well with our transportation professional who grabbed me by the collar. Though I was experiencing inner turmoil, I didn't flinch. Instead, I delivered a true British response to an attempted assault "Yeah, go on. Hit me. Then I can call the police and file a charge for bodily assault."

Faced with this devastating combination of logic and legal threats, the driver backed down and drove off into the night, leaving Julie and I standing on the curb victorious, if slightly inconvenienced.

8

My Life in Vietnam

There is an anecdote credited to Oliver Cromwell, an English military and political leader who was the Lord Protector of England, Scotland, and Ireland from 1653 until his death in 1658. This was just after the English Civil War (1642-1651). While sitting for a portrait, he was reported to have told the artist to paint him as he was, "warts and all" rather than idealising him with artistic grandeur as most leaders would have requested. I'll bet that was a bit unusual for the times, but Cromwell's idea of depicting a person honestly, as they truly are and not as they wished they were, took hold.

Writing this memoir has reminded me just how hard it is to tell the unvarnished truth about yourself, to allow the warts to be addressed. But in order to tell the story of my life as accurately as possible, I have been forced to recognise and remember some painful and embarrassing parts of my past. I had to recall them, think them through, and write them down. And while, I have perhaps glossed over a few warts to save embarrassment to myself and others, I can say with great confidence that today, in the present, I am a very lucky man. I am blessed. Early last year, my wife was diagnosed with cola-rectal cancer but fortunately has come through some extensive surgery well and has been given the all-clear. Even just within the past few months, I have experienced consecutively sheer joy, appreciation, fun, and even awe. In July of 2024, my family and I had a summer cruise round the Baltics and then spent a few days with my daughter Claire, her husband, and my two granddaughters in the UK before returning to Vietnam. Last August, I travelled to England to meet up with my son Jim who had bought hospitality football tickets to watch our beloved Manchester United at Old Trafford getting their arses handed to them 3-0 by Liverpool. The match result was not too joyful, but being at Old Trafford with my eldest son brought back memories of matches we watched together when he was growing up. This made it a wonderful day. On the same trip, we shared an afternoon and evening with my daughter and I spent an entire day with my youngest granddaughter who was staying with her aunt in Manchester. In August, I was given tickets by a close friend to watch the Singapore Grand Prix. For Christmas, Suong, Michael, and I went to our favourite haunt in Phu Quoc, Vietnam's largest island and a delightful holiday retreat. Over the lunar new year holiday, Tet, we stayed in Saigon because Suong likes to spend time with her family. I have no explanation for how I, a cancer survivor of thirty-five years who has been in four serious long-term relationships, could be so lucky. I'm not at all sure how it happened, but it did, and for that I am very appreciative.

Warts and all, I'm doing okay, but it wasn't always thus.

Vietnam also wasn't always like it is today.

With Jim at Manchester United in August 2024

A lot has happened to both myself and my newly adopted country since I first arrived in the early 1990s. A quick history might be helpful for readers who are new to Vietnam.

In 2025, Vietnam celebrated the fiftieth anniversary of the country's liberation and unification. *Doi Moi* in the same year was just one year shy of its 40th birthday. Over these decades, Vietnam has endured several crises such as the American Embargo (lifted in 1994), global and regional economic crises (1997 and 2008), and two global epidemics (SARS and Covid). Despite these significant challenges, the country has thrived. Among many other positive trends and impacts, the *Doi Moi* policies stand out. Launched in 1986, they led to around thirty years of consistent GDP growth and double-digit trade growth. The extreme poverty rate (defined by the World Bank as people living on less than $2 per day) has declined from over 58 percent in 1992 to less than two percent today. Vietnam launched a stock market in July 2000 with just two companies listed, and today the shares of over 400 companies are traded on three separate exchanges in Vietnam — the Ho Chi Minh City stock exchange (HOSE), the Hanoi stock exchange (HNX), and the Unlisted Public Company Market (UPCOM). In 2007, Vietnam joined the World Trade Organization, and it currently has bilateral trade agreements with sixteen separate countries and trading blocks. At the time of this writing in March 2025, Vietnam anticipates that its classification by global rating agencies will change before too long from frontier market to emerging market. This will put Vietnam on the radar screen of global investors in a way it has so far been unable to do. At its 13th Congress in January 2021, the Party announced its goal of making Vietnam a high-income country by 2045. The GDP growth rate has averaged more than 6 percent per year for the past two decades, even including the Covid years. The world is changing fast, and the future is not certain nor can anything be taken for granted, but there are reasons to be optimistic given the accomplishments and progress achieved. It is difficult to determine precisely what event or policy has been most important in the process of change, but from my front row seat, I would point to the following factors as being key:

Enterprise and Foreign Investment Laws—In 1987, Vietnam's National Assembly began its journey to attract foreign direct investment (FDI) with the passage of the Foreign Investment Law. It laid out a general framework for foreign companies to set up businesses within Vietnam. It has been revised, for the better, numerous times. In addition, the National Assembly passed a series of domestic investment and enterprise laws to allow Vietnamese to set up privately-owned commercial businesses. These laws, too, have been revised numerous times (also for the better) over the past three decades. While not always clear or comprehensive, the Vietnamese government fairly quickly set up the legal means for commercial companies, both foreign and domestic, to do business. This was in the *Doi Moi* era beginning in the early 1990s as well as in the current era with the government's new campaign of '*Era of National Rise.*' Today, a Vietnamese citizen can get a company established and incorporated under Vietnamese law within a week or two.

Normalization of USA-Vietnam Diplomatic Relations—The impact of the draconian US Embargo policy on Vietnam cannot be over-stated. It created problems that I was forced to deal with constantly. If the embargo had really been a bilateral issue, meaning only between the United States and Vietnam, it may not have had as negative of an impact as it did. But the US forced its allies and many global institutions to follow its lead in isolating and punishing Vietnam. After the fall of the Berlin Wall in 1989, the communist regimes in many East European countries collapsed, and Vietnam was left with very few allies or supporting countries for trade and investment. When the US embargo was finally lifted in February 1994, nearly two decades after the end of the war, the country was suddenly open for business to the world. Normalisation of full diplomatic relations between the USA and Vietnam occurred in 1995 which further integrated Vietnam into the global economy. From that point forward, the GDP of Vietnam grew on average by about 6.5 percent a year for the next 25 years.

The Stock Market(s)—In July 2000, the Ho Chi Minh City stock exchange (HOSE) opened with two state-owned companies list, REE (an industrial engineering and refrigeration company) and SACOM (a telecommunications equipment company). 'Equitization' was the official word used to describe the process of state-owned companies becoming privately-held joint stock shareholding companies that consisted of shares owned by management, employees, and outside investors. When REE and SACOM were listed, existing shareholders, including employees, could sell their shares and receive the full sale price. In addition, outside investors not connected to either company could also become shareholders. VinaMilk, Sacom Bank and the Saigon Petroleum Construction Company were listed shortly after the first two companies, and during its first year of operation, the HOSE was the fastest-growing stock market in the world. Today, HOSE has a market cap of around US$ 200 billion and is heading for an upgrade from Frontier to Emerging Market status.

US-Vietnam bilateral trade agreement—One of the very

first shared objectives between Vietnam and United States after political normalisation was to negotiate a bilateral trade agreement. The agreement that finally emerged in July 2000 from the negotiations was detailed and comprehensive, and it went into effect in December 2001. Trade had already been ongoing at higher tariff rates, but the new agreement provided an immediate boost with Vietnamese exports to the USA spiking by 300 percent in the first full year after the agreement went live. In 2001, bilateral trade between the two nations totalled $1.9 billion, and by the end of 2024, it had increased to nearly $150 billion. In addition, the agreement addressed numerous other areas of business which assuaged many concerns among US companies which wanted to invest in Vietnam. American FDI also grew strongly from this point on.

Consolidation and Equitization of State-Owned Enterprises—During the late 1990s and early 2000s, the Vietnamese economy was still dominated by state-owned enterprises (SOEs). Many of the FDI projects were also joint ventures between SOEs and foreign companies and few of them truly succeeded. At the time, there were around 6,000 SOEs in Vietnam. Over time, there was an acceptance by the government that Vietnam's SOEs were too big, too inefficient, too redundant, and too expensive to keep them all afloat. Therefore, there was an effort to consolidate as many of them as possible. There was also an effort to 'equitize' (that is, convert the firms into shareholding companies) as many of them as possible in order to improve their profitability and sustainability. The strongest among them were fully equitized and eventually got listed on the stock exchanges. This era was significant because Vietnamese government planners consciously avoided trying to keep SOEs alive through subsidies and market protection. Instead, they forced many of them them to move towards competing in the market on their own merits.

The Rise of the Private Sector—While the SOE sector was undergoing consolidation, reform, and equitization, the country's private sector was starting to boom. An Enterprise Law in 1999 built on the domestic investment law of 1994 began to ease the way for local entrepreneurs to build companies and compete head-to-head with SOEs and foreign-invested companies. Many of them started out as joint stock companies with multiple shareholders. Thus, they could more easily seek out initial public offerings (IPOs) on the country's stock exchanges. The combination of forcing SOEs to compete and allowing private sector companies to grow and raise capital meant the business economy of Vietnam became more akin to any market economy country in the world.

Vietnam's entry into the World Trade Organization—Building on the experience gained from negotiating the US-Vietnam Bilateral Trade Agreement, Vietnam was fairly well prepared to begin the process required to join the World Trade Organization (WTO). This occurred on January 1, 2007. Among other benefits, it meant Vietnam was fully integrated into the global economy. In some ways, this moment could be considered the starting point for Vietnam's growth and development for the next few decades.

The above events and factors all significantly impacted the country's social and economic well-being. Because of these policies and outcomes, Vietnam progressed to a point where it could effectively address a range of issues that would most likely have been dealt with differently, and possibly poorly, or not at all, if not for *Doi Moi*.

These challenges include:

Vietnam's Fight Against Covid—Vietnam had two separate battles against the Covid-19 pandemic. It succeeded exceptionally

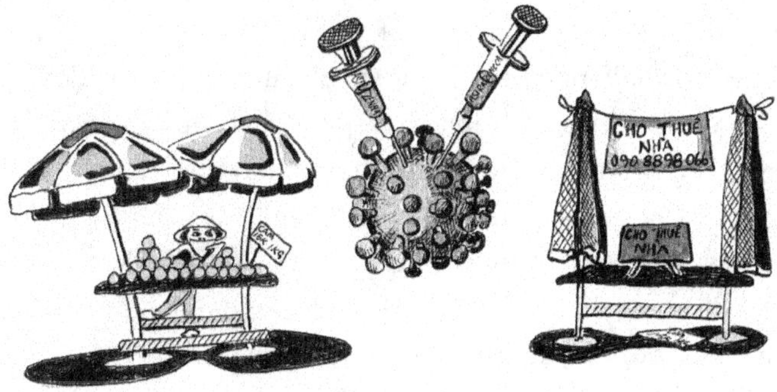

well in its first battle and responded relatively well in its second battle. In both cases, the government responded quite quickly on a policy and action plan to compel the country's 100 million citizens to respond to a pandemic whose source was less than 1,500 kilometres away (the driving distance between Wuhan China and the northern border of Vietnam). The two separate battles and their outcomes are worth noting in this memoir as examples of what Vietnam was able to accomplish in the most trying of circumstances.

The first battle coincided with the outbreak of Covid-19 at the beginning of 2020. In the early stages, the coronavirus was spreading across Europe, but there were no deaths and very few contractions within Vietnam. But the government still responded quickly, closing all schools in February 2020 and ceasing all air transportation to and from China. This was followed by a ban on all international commercial air transport in and out of Vietnam starting in March 2020. Normal flights did not resume for two years, though regulated repatriation and emergency flights were permitted. By the end of 2020, by which time 83 million people around the world had contracted the disease with 1.8 million people dying from it, there were only around 1,500 cases of Covid 19 in all of Vietnam and just 35 Covid-related deaths.

The second battle, which began in May 2021, involved the Delta and Omicron variants of Covid-19. This posed a more significant challenge because it spread much more quickly and the government was not able to respond fast enough. In addition, it had not yet launched a vaccine campaign due, in part, to there being so few cases in the first battle against Covid. Also there was no locally manufactured vaccines available. However, the government quickly launched a campaign and instituted a lockdown of nearly all aspects of normal life. Within several months, it vaccinated more than 80 percent of the population against Covid and in most cases administered a booster shot as well. By end of 2022, Vietnam had recorded around 11.5 million Covid cases that resulted in 43,186 deaths. While obviously tragic, it was comparatively better off than many countries. The United States, for instance, over the same time frame reported over 100 million cases and 1.1 million virus-related deaths.

Bamboo Diplomacy—Since the first Trump administration began its trade war with China in 2018, Vietnam has received a lot of global attention. As a border country with 100 million people and a labor force of 60 million, Vietnam is well positioned to benefit from the new Cold War on trade between the two largest economies in the world. To do this well, it must finesse a highly delicate series of political and economic relationships with two very different countries. Rather than side with one country over the other, Vietnam chose to side with neither and to look out for its own interests. It's even given this diplomatic approach a name, "Bamboo Diplomacy."

There are and have been several examples of Bamboo Diplomacy. One was visible on the front pages of every major newspaper in Vietnam and even several international newspapers on two separate occasions in late 2023. The first occasion was when US President Joe Biden visited Vietnam in September 2023 to sign a Comprehensive Strategic Partnership (CSP) agreement with Vietnam. The country's newspapers published page one photos of President Biden and General Secretary Nguyen Phu Trong shaking hands and smiling. Approximately eight weeks later, Chinese President Xi Jinping visited Vietnam in November 2023 to sign similar agreements. For that visit, the Vietnamese media published an almost identical photo of General Secretary Nguyen Phu Trong shaking hands and smiling, but this time with President Xi. It's hard to imagine a similar set of photos being published during the first Cold War between the USA and the USSR.

Trade Agreements and Comprehensive Strategic Partnerships—A continuation of Bamboo Diplomacy and an interesting 'growth area' for Vietnam has been the number of countries in the world for which it has developed trade and diplomatic relations. As of this writing in early 2025, Vietnam is party to 15 bilateral trade agreements (BTAs). It is also part of trade consortiums with the ASEAN nations, the European Union, and it invested 10 years to join the Trans-Pacific Partnership (TPP). The TPP was an agreement among 12 nations of the Asia Pacific, including Vietnam, who established a set of rules for trade and investment. On day four of the Trump Administration in 2017, the USA withdrew from the TPP and the remaining 11 countries re-grouped in 2018 to form the Comprehensive and Progressive Agreement for Trans-Pacific Partnership (CPTPP). The UK's membership, sponsored by Vietnam, was ratified in December 2024.

Another growing group is the number of countries with which Vietnam has a 'Comprehensive Strategic Partnership' agreement. For several years, this designation was the realm of just three countries (China, Russia, and India) and it shaped how the countries dealt with and negotiated with each other. By the end of March 2025, the number of countries with the same status grew to 12. The total list and date of these agreements are: China (May 2008), Russia (July 2012), India (September 2016), South Korea (December 2022), United States (September 2023), Japan (November 2023), Australia (March 2024), France (October 2024), Malaysia (November 2024), New Zealand (February 2025), Indonesia (March 2025), and Singapore (March 2025). In each case, there is an extensive and detailed agreement that each country pledges to abide by and includes issues like trade, investment, technology transfer, diplomacy, education exchanges, environmental objectives and other key issues. Ultimately, this is a measurement of how engaged a country is and, by this metric, Vietnam is becoming more and more engaged with the world.

In the latter half of 2024, Vietnam had some significant leadership transitions. Its 'Blazing Furnace' anti-corruption campaign had netted some very big fish and replacements for those posts had to be identified and placed into power. This was a difficult task. One of the negative impacts of the anti-corruption campaign was a slowdown in public investment for many projects that had already been approved and already had the funds made available for investment and distribution. The department heads and senior management for these projects were too hesitant to sign off on the projects for fear of retribution if something went wrong or if someone on the project team had been involved with corruption in the past. Rather than sign off on a project that had been approved, the safer course was to wait it out. Of course, having to prove a negative is always difficult and thus projects became stalled.

General Secretary Nguyen Phu Trong died in July 2024 and the eventual ascendancy of To Lam took some time. For a few months, Mr. Lam held both the Presidency and the General Secretary role which was a major change for some people inside and outside of Vietnam. Since the introduction of *Doi Moi* in 1986, Vietnam has always had a four-pillar power structure of the General Secretary, President, Prime Minister, and Chairman of the National Assembly being held by four different individuals. There was an 18-member Politburo, a 200-member Central Committee, and a 500-member National Assembly. Every five years, there was a National Party Congress of around 1,600 delegates, including the above-mentioned members, who discussed, debated, and signed off on the policies for the next five years of growth and development. This was the political status quo and it was stable. When Mr. Lam held two positions simultaneously, this was out of the political norm. However, within a couple of months, a new President had been approved by the National Assembly and Vietnam's politically stable Four Pillar structure was back in place.

As Vietnam began the year 2025, there appeared to be a concerted effort to launch a new round of reforms being labelled the '*Era of National Rise*.' Some pundits and political watchers have labeled it as *Doi Moi* 2.0. There have been official government announcements regarding institutional reform including the merging of 63 cities and provinces to 34 and the consolidation and merger of several government ministries. The goal is a more stream-lined government system that has a better chance of achieving the eight percent or 10 percent GDP growth rate that Prime Minister Pham Minh Chinh announced for the year 2025.

Can all of this be done? Time will tell. What I can say is that I closely follow it all and consider myself lucky to have worked and lived in Vietnam through all these changes. I played a role in some of them and am proud of my contribution and my work. It's been quite a journey with a lot of ups and downs.

As I wrote above, I moved to Vietnam on a permanent basis in 1993. However, I still travelled frequently to Hong Kong. One trip in particular is one that I can never forget.

In late December 1995, I was visiting Julie, my girlfriend at the time, in Hong Kong. We were planning to celebrate the Christmas and New Year's holidays together before I went back to Vietnam. For unknown reasons at the time, I had a massive blood loss. Julie refused to let me get on a plane until I saw a doctor. We went to a clinic and they referred me to a hospital where they did a bunch of tests. This was over a couple of days just after Christmas. Shortly afterwards, we got the call to come in and talk with a surgeon.

"Do you want the good news or the bad news first?" he asked.

"Give me the good news first," I said.

"Well, the good news is that I think we can do something about it. The bad news is you have cancer. We are going to have to do surgery immediately," he said.

I asked if he thought I would die between then (December 28) and January 1. He said no, but wanted to know why that was important.

"I have tickets for a New Year's Eve party. If it's going to be my last one, I want to go," I told him. I negotiated a deal with him to postpone the surgery until January 3 if I promised to walk five kilometres a day, eat nothing but red meat, and do strenuous breathing exercises. The doctor explained that he wanted a lot of red meat in my diet because he knew I was going to lose a lot of blood during the operation and red meat has high iron content. I kept up my end of the bargain by walking and eating red meat and doing the breathing exercises, and I also had one hell of a lot of fun at the New Year's Eve party at the Hong Kong Football Club. After eight hours of surgery on January 3, I came out of it okay. I survived the cancer, went back to Vietnam and immediately got back to work trying to figure out how to make a living in a country where it was notoriously difficult to make money.

Julie and I got married in 2000, but sadly we separated in 2003. I was still cancer free, but I really went downhill after the break-up. Julie had pulled me through the cancer years, the Vietnam business building years, and now I was on my own. I was out every night, drinking way too much, and doing things I shouldn't have been doing. I was at rock bottom.

That was when Lady Luck, or whatever you want to call it, arrived with two gifts. First, I met Suong. I was out as usual with my drinking buddies. She was out with a group of women friends for one of her girlfriend's birthdays. We made eye contact, chatted a bit, and I got her phone number. I called her the next day and very soon we were dating. Less than a year later, we had moved in together. Later on, we got married and have been married for more than 15 years. When we first got married, I was adamant about not having children and I told her that very clearly. Suong agreed, but a few years later, as fate does to people sometimes, she changed her mind and said she wanted to have a child. I changed my mind, too, and I'm so, so grateful that I did. We have Michael, and I'm in an emotional and financial space where I can provide for him the kind of life that I wish I could have provided for Jim and Claire. We're a close-knit family. Some days I take him to school, but I'm almost always home when he comes back from school and we share about our day. It's wonderful.

The second gift that I received about the same time that I met Suong was getting invited by California Fitness, a new client for Grant Thornton, to join a body transformation contest. Aside from having a great new client, this opened up a whole new opportunity for me to get healthy. One of the trainers, a guy called Al Morgan, knocked me into shape boot camp style! I still go there every week. I have a trainer and a pretty strict fitness plan. I work out at least three mornings a week, have lunch, and do some work in the afternoon while waiting for Michael to finish school. In terms of workload, I have slowed down a little bit but not that much. I am now just an advisor to Grant Thornton, but I sit on a number of other boards as an independent director. I love this, as I can contribute to a company based on my experience building Grant Thornton in Vietnam and my many other experiences, while also learning about new business sectors. The stress associated with work is mostly gone mainly because there are no staff reports to read, no KPIs to hit, and no top or bottom line responsibilities. Sometimes, I have to read a few hundred pages of reports to prepare for a board meeting, but that's about it. My work and life balance is pretty good. I earn enough now through board of director compensation and bonuses on various projects to maintain the life style that I had before "retirement," and I really enjoy the opportunity to share what I have learned from my business career.

I am still on the Board of BritCham and I am still Vice Chairman of the Vietnam Tourism Advisory Board. I keep busy. I am not sure if I'll ever retire. In fact, I'm not even sure what that word means anymore, because I have no idea what I would do with myself if I wasn't working. Like some of my colleagues have shared about me, work is my hobby. At the spritely young age of 76, I am a happy family man who has been blessed with a second chance at parenthood and living the good life.

It took a while to get to this point, though.

My first proper home in Vietnam was in 1993 in a neighbourhood that we called "the ghetto." Today, it's more commonly called Japan Town because of all the Japanese restaurants, but it could also be called "Massage Town" because

of all the massage parlours. Back then, it was a rabbit warren of villa type homes in a couple of lanes just off Le Thanh Ton Street in D1. The houses were often four meters wide and 20 meters deep and from two to five floors in height with the fifth floor generally being a rooftop garden of some kind. They lined up right next to each other. I recall my place being six meters wide, but it was cozy to say the least. My 'alarm clock' was my neighbour who would start up his Vespa motorcycle early every morning just outside my door and drive off to work. I could walk to my office in the morning and there were three or four bars in between to drop in for a drink on my way home.

To be honest, the consultancy business was slow, and to create another income stream we set up a parallel agency and distribution business. We brought in companies such as Diversey (Diversey Lever today) Frigoscandia, Scala accounting software, Southcorp wines from Australia, and Boddingtons from the UK. We hired three mature graduates from the Asia Pacific Business program run by Capilano College in Canada. These postgraduates had to do a one-year internship, which meant we could afford to hire them. They did a great job and two of them remained with us after the internship. David who ran the Diversey agency proceeded to have a great career in Asia, mainly in Thailand. As the consulting business developed, and Grant Thornton was requiring auditing services in Vietnam, some of these agencies terminated and some such as Diversey were sold to a close friend, Mark Gillen of AIM and he still operates them to this today.

As I have written before, I hate to eat alone and I rarely ended up doing so back in the early and mid-1990s. Though there are many more bar and restaurant options today, it was a great time to live and work in Saigon. Among my favourite haunts were the Q Bar, which was a great bar right below the Opera House and of course the Floating Hotel. I had the pleasure of being invited to have lunch at 'The Floater,' as we called it, by Patrick Imbardelli the day before it officially opened. I was also there in 1996 to see it depart with all its history and unspoken stories. The Q bar has been closed for quite a while now so only long-term expats and a certain group of Vietnamese who liked to hang out with foreigners would remember the place. Back in the 1990s, it was the place to go along with the Apocalypse Now bar and the Down Under disco on the Floating Hotel. Sean and An, the owners, are now neighbours of mine in City Garden where my family and I live today [sadly An passed away at the time of finishing this Memoir]. It was quite common to have cocktails and pre-dinner drinks at the Q Bar, go out to eat, and then we would end up at Apocalypse Now or the Down Under until God knows what time. Those places never seemed to close and it really got hopping around midnight. Man, those were fun times.

In terms of dining, the Camargue restaurant was probably the most popular amongst my group of friends. It featured Mediterranean cuisine and had a fairly extensive wine list for the time. One of my first business partners, Alexander Egert, ran the place. There were really good Vietnamese street food restaurants all over the place along with many more formal restaurants. In the back of the Islamic Mosque on Dong Du street, there was a small restaurant where they cooked for the staff and anyone else who ventured in. They served Halal beef, chicken curry, and other Indian dishes for lunch, at a cost of perhaps US$2. They did a booming business because it was good, inexpensive, and in a great location. Back then, there were few Japanese and Korean places, which reflected the relatively low number of expats living in Saigon. A few of the foreign restaurants were owned by citizens of those countries who had moved to Vietnam and become restaurant entrepreneurs. They had their own specialised supply chains for local and imported ingredients to satisfy their countrymen's palate. If you had even a bit of money in your pocket (and actually even if you were broke), it was impossible to go hungry.

In those early days, as I was trying to get something solid set up in terms of business, I couldn't help but compare Vietnam to China. I had left China knowing it had become too big for a private consultancy of my size. I had focused on Vietnam because I believed and hoped that it would be different. It would be a better fit for someone like myself. One big difference was not so much between the countries, but with the work that I was doing. In China, I was representing foreign investors and companies who wanted to do business there. My job was to help them get started and I was paid for this work. Whether they made money or not, I still got paid because of the consulting contract. When I tried to start up my own business in Vietnam, it was different. Of course, I still needed clients, but Vietnam was a very new market. It didn't have the population or the appeal of China and therefore it did not have a bunch of multi-national corporations eager to jump in and do business. For this reason, I needed to figure out how to make money beyond a consulting role for a large foreign corporation.

One difference that I quickly learned about was the cultural and historical differences between China and Vietnam. In China, whenever I wanted to set up a meeting with a high government official, I had to practically come in on my knees as if I was kowtowing to the emperor. The government official was an emperor of sorts, but just for his own province which could be as large as 100 million people. This was part of the Mandarin bureaucracy system. Even leaders from poor provinces could demand this kind of behaviour from investors or anyone else who was seeking to do business in their province. It was a face thing.

Vietnam was very different in this regard. If we wanted to get a meeting with someone like the Secretary to the Council of Ministers or the head of the State Committee for Cooperation and Investment (SCCI), this could be arranged. I would just need to have had previous access or one or two fixer types and a meeting could be scheduled. In general, the Vietnamese were a lot more easy-going and friendly. There was not a lot of foreign direct investment coming into Vietnam in the early 1990s. For this reason, a lot of these officials were more than happy to meet and were genuinely curious about foreign companies and what foreign investors could do for the country. It was all very new to them and they were eager to learn. Starting in the early 1990s, I was able to build a *guanxi* (connections) network in Vietnam and it's a network that I have to this day. I also had *guanxi* in China, and in some cases with some very high-level officials, but in the end my *guanxi* didn't make my China ventures all that successful. If they had been successful, I doubt that I would have ever left.

Friendly bureaucrats, though, do not a profitable business make. It was extremely precarious in those early days. I often spoke at investor conferences and I had a few canned jokes that I would always use to introduce Vietnam to the audience. The attendees were mostly newcomers who were curious about investing in Vietnam. One was the standard phrase of "It's a marathon, not a sprint" which pretty much everyone working here knew. The other joke, which almost always got some nervous laughs, was "How do you become a millionaire in Vietnam? You arrive as a billionaire or exchange a US$100 bill." [and become a Vietnam Dong multi-millionaire!].

It was tough. I recall an uncomfortable conversation with Julie about our future in Vietnam. This was in 1996. I/we had around $5,000 left in the bank. The monthly payroll was around $3,000. After paying all the staff, we would have enough for two tickets out and wouldn't be able to make payroll the following month. She asked if I had a Plan B in mind. Go back to Hong Kong? Go back to England? I didn't have a Plan B. I only had Plan A, which was to build a business in Vietnam. I loved living in Saigon. The people, the atmosphere, the food and drinks... the energy was great. I was living a good life, but I needed something solid and stable if I wanted to stay. In 1994, we had become a correspondent firm for Grant Thornton International and by 1997 they were pressuring me to establish an audit practice and become a full member firm.

That's when a lawyer friend and Hanoi drinking buddy, Mark Lockwood, told me about a small Australian accounting firm called Bourne Griffiths. He encouraged me to reach out to them.

"Reach out about what?" I asked. "I'm not an accountant."

"So what?" he replied. "This is Vietnam. You know the project finance industry as well as anyone in this country and you can learn accounting."

At the end of Chapter Seven, I mentioned that I had set up a Hong Kong company which I named Project Consultancy Services or PCS. This was a legal entity for doing business in Asia. For the Vietnam market, I sought out a local partner with intentions of setting up what its called a Business Cooperation Contract, or BCC, which is an arrangement that allows for a foreign company to work with a Vietnamese company investors in business activities without forming a new legal entity. It's a convenient way for a foreign company to operate in Vietnam, and I have over the years arranged quite a number of them for clients. To get it done, I needed a local company to contract with, and as recounted earlier, I found the right partner in Cho Lon Import Export Company or Cholimex. It had a very long history in the old China Town district of Saigon, known as Cholon. So in 1993, we set up the BCC between PCS and Cholimex with the mandate of doing project consulting. With this structure in place, I was allowed to do officially consulting work and could invoice work through the BCC. This made my life a bit easier, but simply having a BCC didn't necessarily lead to any business and clients. I had to find those on my own.

It was during this time that I was able to procure the franchise rights from Grant Thornton, an international accounting firm that did not have a presence in Vietnam. I pursued that because I anticipated that Vietnam would eventually be of interest to more and more global companies and because Grant Thornton's business model was a membership franchise model. This meant that only one franchise member of the Grant Thornton network could set up in Vietnam, and I wanted to be that member if and when they decided that Vietnam was of interest. Of the Big Four international accounting firms, only Ernst and Young was operating in Vietnam at that point, and I felt that if I played my cards right, we could become one of the leaders. So in 1994, we became a correspondent firm for the Grant Thornton network.

IN 1994 shortly after I got the BCC license with Cholimex through a relationship with a Grant Thornton Partner from Hong Kong, I was asked if we would like to join the Grant

Thornton Network which was a member firm network (similar to a franchise). At the time I was actually talking to the global accounting firm network PKF, as they had a strong tourism and hospitality practice. But because of relationships and other people I knew in the GT world, I opted for Grant Thornton because I saw the value of having that as a brand name. In addition, because we did not have an audit practice, we could be a correspondent firm so the annual fee was only something like US$500 per annum.

We had to go through an incoming firms review but because of my banking background, we had a procedures manual covering all aspects of the business and a template for all client files, and we passed with flying colours. However, they did not understand our agency structure, which was a means to making our ends meet. So before I attended my first global conference, which happened to be in Hong Kong, I had to be interviewed by GT's International board of directors, whose members thankfully approved our membership. That conference was an eye-opener, with partners from over 60 countries present, and we got on with most like a house on fire. I instantly knew I had made the right call.

The challenge came in 1997 when the pressure was on to become a full member firm and being able to provide audit services. Enter Bourne Griffiths the following year, and I re-organised everything.

I had a few things to bring to the party. I had a Hong Kong based company, I had my own personal experience and network within Vietnam from which I could hustle up work, and I had an office and staff under the existing BCC with Cholimex. I had the desire to stick it out in Vietnam and make things work. And maybe most crucially for the future, I had the Grant Thornton membership in my possession. On the Bourne Griffiths side, it was an established Australian accounting firm with fully-certified accountants, and it had a local auditing license. It also had a few Australian customers. What it lacked, in my view, was someone like myself to bring business through the door and also some funds for business development. I realised that to make this deal work I would have to come up with some capital to keep the new ship afloat, but I personally didn't have any money.

So what did I do? First, I borrowed enough money from my Mum to buy a stake in Bourne Griffiths, and I am glad to say that I managed to pay it all back within a couple of years.

With an ownership stake in the Vietnam-based Bourne Griffiths which had an established office in Vietnam, I terminated the BCC arrangement with Cholimex and continued my consulting business through Bourne Griffiths. Effectively, I merged PCS with Bourne Griffiths and kept their name on the understanding that we would change the name to Grant Thornton as soon as we could. The basic agreement was that I would do consulting work and keep a percentage of the profits. The original and any new Bourne Griffiths staff who were qualified to do so, would continue to do accounting and auditing work. I was now a part-owner of an accounting firm, but I still did not have any credentials as an accountant.

This turned out to be a good move. It gave me a legal entity in Vietnam in which I was a part owner. Though I wasn't an accountant, I was surrounded by accountants and could add value to numerous clients on the consulting side. I also had my own consulting clients, many of whom had need of accounting and auditing services. Most importantly, we were able to respond to Grant Thornton International's questions about setting up an auditing practice in Vietnam. We changed the name of Bourne Griffiths to Grant Thornton in 1998. I eventually did become a Vietnamese CPA in 2012 after having become a member of CPA Australia in 2011.

However, in 1998 and 1999, we needed to get a few quick wins on the board to get the company financially viable. Through one of my good contacts in Hanoi, we were alerted to a major capacity building project funded by the Asian Development Bank (ADB) and involving the State Bank of Vietnam, the Ministry of Finance, and the State Securities Commission. It was the biggest project we had ever seen in Vietnam. It involved building the capacity for the equitization process (meaning the privatisation of SOEs) and would require 15 to 20 experienced consultants for a year. The budgeted fees were in excess of US$ 1.5 million. My contact helped arrange a dinner meeting with some officials from the Ministry of Finance.

Grant Thornton had to get on the short list, and the dinner meeting was the first step towards getting that done. We had to get this one right. My contact set up the meeting at a seafood restaurant in Hanoi with a small group of Ministry of Finance officials. During the dinner, I talked about myself, the potential project, about the strengths of Grant Thornton, and in general did my usual networking thing. I felt the dinner meeting was going well. I could answer their queries and posed good questions to them. I was connecting together everyone at the table. My friend whispered to me that they liked me, but were worried that Grant Thornton was too small and unknown to take on such a large project. This was a common concern with many large multilateral projects. The big accounting and consulting firms tended to win such contracts because they could offer a huge list of completed projects and qualified individuals who could be put to work on such a project. We were too new to be able to match that kind of pitch, so as the conversation started to wind down, I decided to try a new angle.

"So," I asked the group, "who is your favourite football team?"

"Manchester United," they all said almost simultaneously. The mood of the dinner definitely picked up. I perked up, too.

"Really? Me too. In fact, I am from Manchester," I replied. "Also, Grant Thornton is the auditor for the Manchester United football club."

The mood instantly changed. It was as if Sir Alex Ferguson had suddenly appeared and sat down at our table. They all leaned forward eager to talk about football. The equitization project was forgotten, and instead, we ordered whiskey and talked about sports and the power of football well into the night. My new angle worked. We got on the short list and, ultimately, we won the tender. We successfully worked on the project for a year and delivered our results. The Asian Development Bank declared it to be their best-managed project in all of Asia. One year later, after winning the bid for ADB project, I recounted this tale to my Grant Thornton colleagues at our annual global conference, and I learned then that KPMG had actually taken over the Manchester United auditing contract the prior year, around the time of my dinner with the MOF. I had made my successful pitch to the Ministry of Finance, with the claim that Grant Thornton was the official auditor of the football club, and it was almost true. I sold them on the fact that GT were the auditors and in fact at the time they had just lost the audit, but I did not know. In life, timing is everything, sports is a great unifier, and ignorance is sometimes bliss.

In 1999 I had learnt that Grant Thornton Spain were auditors to Barcelona football club and though the Managing Partner I was able to secure two tickets for the epic European Champions League final when Manchester United played Bayern Munich in the Neu Camp. I flew from Vietnam to Barcelona for one night via Hong Kong, London, and Madrid and fortunately because of Grant Thornton's relationship with the club, I managed to secure

Sir Bobby Charlton and I at Vasco's Restaurant in Saigon in 1998

a room in a hotel owned by the President of the club walking distance from the ground. I was accompanied by my good friend Jeremy Bayfield who was a travel agent who managed a lot of the travel for the BBC and who often helped get tickets for Jim and I to see Man United Games, so I was able to repay a favour. What a night it was! United had already won the League and the FA Cup and were going for the historic treble. We had great seats and about almost on the centre line and behind the VIP seats and Garry Lineker was seated just in front of us. It was an amazing feeling watching the likes of Peter Schmeichel, Gary Neville, Jaap Stam, Denis Irwin David Beckham, Nicky Butt, Ryan Giggs, Dwight Yorke, and Andy Cole running onto the pitch in the amazing Neu Camp stadium. The first 85 minutes were a disaster, United were one nil down and did not look like scoring until Ferguson substituted Teddy Sheringham and Ole Gunnar Solskjaer for Andy Cole and Blomquist. I remember thinking it was all over when Gary Lineker left the ground at 85 minutes.

You cannot imagine the eruption when Sheringham scored in the first minute of added time. I could not believe it and in fact I was still jumping up and down when Ole Gunnar scored in the 93rd minute with almost the last kick of the game! The United fans were jubilant and could not believe it – two goals in three minutes and the poor Bayern fans who had seen their team's colours being put onto the cup only to have them removed. Then it was onto Las Ramblas for a celebration, before starting the long journey home the next morning. This experience certainly gave me the bug for the big games, and following that I went to the final in Moscow in 2008 when Man United beat Chelsea on penalties, Rome in 2009 where we lost to Barcelona and 2011 at Wembley where we lost to Barcelona again.

The ADB project really boosted our fortunes, both in terms of business (i.e., revenue) and reputation. We were off and running as an accounting, auditing and business consultancy and capacity building firm. Over the next ten plus years (1998 to around 2010), that is the work we did. During this time, several important things happened starting with the opening of modern Vietnam's first stock market in July 2000. Second, the bilateral trade agreement between the USA and Vietnam was put into place in 2001 and third, at the beginning of 2007, Vietnam joined the World Trade Organization. Vietnam also began to negotiate separate bilateral trade agreements with many different countries and trade groups. The Vietnamese economy was growing and Grant Thornton was doing well. One of our key clients was VinaCapital, for which we did auditing work and with which Grant Thornton still has a good relationship today. In addition to the ADB project, we also won a significant consulting contract with the World Bank. Over these years, Grant Thornton grew into a 100-person firm.

It was around 2011 when I was introduced by the CFO of

VinaCapital to a Vietnamese accountant named Nguyen Chi . He was the founder and managing partner of Nexia ACPA, a local accounting firm started up by a group of Vietnamese accountants who had worked at Arthur Anderson and then KPMG after the demise of Anderson globally. They were based mainly in Hanoi but had a small office in Ho Chi Minh City and wanted to expand. They were quite strong in taxation and audit and had a niche client base among Japanese companies. Trung expressed his desire to take Nexia ACPA to "the next level" and he shared the suggestion that forming a merger with an international accounting firm would be the best means to accomplish this goal. We had never met before, but while it was a very cordial first meeting, I couldn't at that point see a merger working. We were about the same size, 100 or so staff each, but I think our revenues were higher. We also still had VinaCapital as an audit customer. I was worried that we would get bogged down in valuations, roles of each side, and other issues. They also had ten equity partners compared to my one, but I was still conscious of the need to put in place a solid succession plan for the firm.

Trung and I had another meeting a couple of years later around 2013. We were still of equal size, but each side had become bigger and we were generating about the same revenues. One big change on our side was losing the VinaCapital account for auditing. Nexia ACPA was strong in taxation and had a good auditing practice. Grant Thornton was strong in advisory matters and also had a good auditing practice. Our largest office was in the south of Vietnam and they were larger in the north. They had a good client base among Japanese companies. We had a good client base among other foreign investors. They were a 100 percent Vietnamese company. We were a foreign-invested company that had a global network behind it. For a whole bunch of reasons, a discussion about a merger this time around made a lot more sense.

Over my career, I had been party to several discussions about mergers on behalf of clients and friends. Based on this experience, I was worried about three issues right from the start. First, would there be significant cultural issues especially considering that Nexia ACPA was entirely a Vietnamese firm? Second, what would the price be and how would each side value themselves compared to the other side? Third, who would be the managing partner, the person in charge of the newly merged entity? These are the important questions that have tanked proposed mergers of companies around the world.

Fortunately, things were not so difficult for us. Culturally, we were almost the same. The premise of Grant Thornton's membership network was based on getting locals to develop the business and the brand. I had already been in Vietnam for two decades and knew my way around. The Nexia Partners had nearly all been trained by Western-based accountants who had started at Arthur Anderson and then moved onto KPMG. There were no concerns about ethics, quality control, or skill sets. In terms of valuation, it was a relatively easy discussion because we were almost identical in size and revenues. Agreeing to a 50-50 valuation was easy. But the issue of who would run the show could have been problematic. Trung was more than capable of being the CEO of the newly merged firm. I probably was as well, but I was also 65 years old and a bit tired of running a big company. I knew this, but the others didn't.

When we arrived at this question during our merger negotiations, I decided to have a bit of fun. Someone finally posed the question of who would be the managing partner. There was a long pause.

"Okay, guys, there's no real discussion on this issue," I told the group. I didn't say anything more, and just looked around the table. There was another uncomfortable (for them) pause. They thought that I was going to demand that I be the CEO. Maybe they were also worried that Grant Thornton International would want to have a say in choosing the CEO and that a Vietnamese national would not be considered. Maybe it had to be a foreigner. I let the pause continue for a while.

"It's got to be Trung," I told the group. I then shared that Grant Thornton's mission was to have local partners in territories all around the world. Our merger, I said, was basically a perfect example of the GT strategy. Trung had taken the initiative to be proactive about growing Nexia to the next level by seeking out a merger. It was his idea and efforts that got us to this point. It was only natural that he be the CEO of the newly enlarged Grant Thornton, which had been doubled in size at the stroke of a pen, and I became the executive chairman. Grant Thornton International later said it was the most successful merger in the history of the brand.

Living in Vietnam has provided me with endless opportunities to build businesses, grow networks and participate in a small way in the growth and development of this country. But it has also provided its fair share of entertainment. Being a stranger in a strange land creates all sorts of opportunities for the strange and the wonderful to occur. A case in point:

In the hustle and bustle of Ho Chi Minh City's Cho Ray Hospital in 2014, I learned an unexpected lesson about Vietnamese hospital etiquette, and the perils of wearing expensive footwear in a sea of flip-flops.

I arrived at the intensive care unit one day to visit my comatose mother-in-law. Following Vietnamese custom, I removed my shoes before entering the ICU. As I placed my polished Barkers leather shoes, undoubtedly worth more than a month's salary for many locals, next to a pile of rubber flip-flops, I had a premonitory thought.

"I wonder if my shoes will still be here when I come out?"

The universe, with its characteristic sense of humour, answered my question with a resounding "No!"

Upon concluding my sombre visit, I emerged to discover my prized Barkers had embarked on an unscheduled journey with an opportunistic new owner. In their place was absolutely nothing, not even a replacement pair of flip-flops nor a courtesy note thanking me for the generous donation to our "family medical fund."

What followed was the kind of walk of shame rarely experienced by corporate executives. Picture the scene: A suit-wearing professional clip-clopping through a Vietnamese hospital in borrowed flip-flops several sizes too small. With the plastic straps digging between my toes, I maintained what dignity I could muster. There were amused glances from the hospital staff who had likely witnessed this scenario play out before.

But rather than fuming over my loss, I chose philosophical resilience. I reasoned that my shoes had been "repurposed" for a greater cause. They were probably sold to fund someone's medical treatment or necessary medications. My expensive Barkers had unwittingly become part of Vietnam's unofficial healthcare subsidy system. As I clip-clopped into the humid Saigon evening, I was left with a uniquely cross-cultural lesson: In Vietnam, sometimes the price of compassion is measured in fine English leather. I was okay with that conclusion.

In the sweltering heat of the dry season of 1998, Vietnam stood on the precipice of its first potential ASEAN Cup football victory against Singapore. For this reason, I found himself caught in what could only be described as Southeast Asia's most alarming victory preparation plan.

I had set out from Ho Chi Minh City to the neighbouring province of Binh Duong to attend a friend's party. Little did I know, I was about to witness what appeared to be the beginnings of World War III. As my hired car cruised along, the unmistakable rumble of heavy machinery announced itself just before a convoy of tanks and military vehicles materialised and thundered down the road towards Ho Chi Minh City like mechanised harbingers of doom.

"Is this the start of another war?" I wondered with visions of historical conflicts flashing before my eyes. Considering Vietnam's 20th century history, one could be forgiven for assuming the worst when faced with a parade of tanks rolling towards a major city.

The truth, as is often the case in Vietnam, was simultaneously more mundane and more wonderfully bizarre than any apocalyptic scenario. These weren't war machines deployed to battle an invading force. They were crowd control measures for potential football celebrations. The Vietnamese authorities, displaying a magnificent blend of passionate football support and a focus on control and safety, had decided that tanks were the appropriate response to potential football revelry.

It's worth pausing here to appreciate the Vietnamese approach to sports celebration management. While other nations might deploy extra police officers or close a few streets, Vietnam was playing 4D chess, sending in the heavy artillery—quite literally—for a football match. This was both a reflection of extreme pessimism about human behaviour and extreme optimism about the national team's chances.

Even more delightfully ironic is what happened next. Vietnam lost the match against Singapore, rendering the tank deployment seemingly unnecessary. However, in a twist that perfectly encapsulates the irrepressible spirit of Vietnamese football fans, the streets erupted in chaotic celebrations anyway! Thousands of motorbikes swarmed the roads, their riders enthusiastically waving the Vietnam flag, honking their horns, and creating the very pandemonium the tanks had been dispatched to control. A sea of jubilant supporters was celebrating what was technically a defeat.

The scene represents the beautiful paradox that is Vietnam. It's a place where authorities might deploy military hardware for a sporting event, and where citizens might celebrate a loss with more fervour than many countries celebrate a win. It's a testament to the unifying power of football that transcends mere victories and defeats. This anecdote encapsulates everything wonderful about Vietnam's relationship with football and its almost religious devotion to the national team. In Vietnam, football isn't just a game—it's a national passion.

At the 2024 ASEAN Cup, Vietnam defeated Thailand for the championship, and the party was on within minutes of the final whistle. No mention of tanks this time. Perhaps the authorities had learned that Vietnamese football fans would react win, lose, or draw, with a harmless carnival.

Another interesting moment came as a result of the fact that for years, people across the UK, France, Hong Kong, and even Vietnam have mistaken me for the British comedy legend Barry Cryer. While most people might find this annoying, I eventually decided to lean into it. And on one occasion, I did so with spectacularly entertaining results.

One day in 2002, I was on board the British Royal Navy's HMS *Nottingham* which was visiting Ho Chi Minh City. Picture the scene: a sophisticated gathering of the British community on a naval vessel, complete with all the pomp and circumstance the Royal Navy can muster. I decided to deliver what might be described as my greatest performance as an international man of comedy.

When a crew member approached me with the familiar question of "Excuse me, are you Barry Cryer?" Inspired by the maritime setting, I decided to abandon my usual straight-laced accountant persona and dived deep into comedic waters.

"Yes, I am," I replied. When asked about my presence in Vietnam, I spun a tale about doing a gig in Singapore (as many famous comedians do) and being invited to Ho Chi Minh City by the British Embassy for the special occasion of the HMS *Nottingham* docking in Saigon. The crew members bought this story hook, line and sinker, or I should say hook, punchline and sinker.

Before long, I found myself invited to the ship's wardroom for drinks, entertaining naval officers with my presence, if not actual jokes. Imagine the pressure of being mistaken for one of Britain's most beloved comedians while trying to maintain witty banter with a room full of sailors. Fortunately, alcohol made everyone funnier.

The evening reached its crescendo when I, having admitted my "Barry Cryer" personae was a joke, invited several crew members to experience Ho Chi Minh City's nightlife. We went to the Apocalypse Now bar even though the sailors had a strict 10 PM curfew imposed on them by Vietnamese authorities. Most of the sailors managed to make it back to the ship on time, proving that the Royal Navy's time-keeping skills remain impeccable even after a few drinks, but one enthusiastic sailor apparently found Vietnam's nightlife too enticing to abandon at the appointed hour. The next morning, he had to be helicoptered back to the ship, a flight paid for by the British Navy. This added a rather expensive exclamation point to my evening of impersonating a comedian. I had somehow managed to turn a case of mistaken identity into an international incident involving the Royal Navy, Vietnamese authorities, and a helicopter rescue, a sequence of events that even the real Barry Cryer himself might have struggled to make up.

But there is another important side to life beyond the business and the extraordinary moments that can come amidst the richness of being a human being, and that is giving back.

A side benefit of being an executive chairman of Grant Thornton Vietnam, instead of the CEO, was that I had more time and freedom to pursue non-business projects, charities, and other work with various social organisations and NGOs. I had been doing this kind of work pretty much since I arrived in Vietnam in the early 1990s. For example, for many years we had a lunch group that met every Friday to talk about both business issues and charity opportunities, and so on. This was before international Chambers of Commerce had been allowed to set up. At the time, the attitude of the Vietnamese government towards the the Chamber of Commerce idea was that Vietnam already had one – the Vietnam Chamber of Commerce and Industry, or VCCI. It was run in those years by an amazing lady named Madam Pham Chi Lan who I had the pleasure of meeting again just recently. One member of our group had a good relationship with her and we in 1996 with her assistance we organised a separate chapter of the VCCI specifically for British businesses. This was the first step towards what eventually became the British Business Group Vietnam or BBGV.

The BBGV operated for a couple years as a chapter of the VCCI because the government had not yet created any regulations covering traditional business groups and allowing foreign chambers of commerce to be established. Back then, there

The British Business Group Vietnam's first office in 1996

also still weren't that many NGOs operating in Vietnam. Then in 1998, some regulations covering chambers were issued and BBGV was transformed into an official chamber. We were the first to be formed. I was secretary in the first year of the BBGV's existence, vice chairman in the second year, and in 1998, the third year, I was appointed chairman, a post I held until 2001. I subsequently had two further stints as chairman of BritCham, which for me was a more formal and organised way to do what I did best, networking and connecting people together. We shared contacts, ideas and information, and basically provided a support network for the local British business community. Vietnam really needed this at the time as did British expats and the expatriate community in general. I still feel very proud of what we accomplished in those years.

One day in the late nineties, my then-wife Julie and I were planning the annual charity ball for the British Business Group of Vietnam. Julie was the director and I was the chairman of the group. This was our keystone event of the year to raise a bunch of money for local charities. In short, it was a big deal and it

With Paul Daniels and Debbie Magee in Saigon in 1998/1999

needed a big act.

Through a British organisation called the Water Rats, we pulled off a remarkable, we can even say 'magical,' coup.

For at least three decades (1970 to 2000), the most famous magician in Great Britain was Paul Daniels. He had his own TV show for more than fifteen years where, before each magic trick, he popularised the phrase, "You'll like this... not a lot, but you'll like this." In 1982, Paul was even awarded Magician of the Year by the Academy of Magical Arts. He sounds a bit like a character in one of the Harry Potter novels, no? The Water Rats, meanwhile, is a charitable organisation of the British entertainment industry, facilitating high level talent to donate their skills to nonprofits and charities around the world, and we managed to negotiate getting Mr. Daniels to come to Vietnam to do a magic show for the BBGV Charity Ball at the New

With Debbie Magee at our house on Pham Ngoc Thach Street

World Hotel. The BBGV had to cover air tickets, hotel costs, and hospitality for Paul and Debbie McGee, who was his assistant and wife. The actual magic show was done for free. We managed to get the flights sponsored and the hotel as well.

The show was amazing. Right at the start, he handed copies of the Bible to three members of the audience, totally random people. He then told them to open the book and start reading a section out loud. He asked them a couple of questions and then shouted out to each person the precise chapter and verse that they were reading. I have no idea how he did that.

Later on, we invited the magical couple to our home for dinner, together with a few close friends. Upon entering our home, Paul warned us that he felt the house was haunted. He then began walking around the house and started knocking on the walls, and someone or something knocked back!

My favourite trick of all those he did took place on the golf course. Now, golf is usually a game of quiet concentration, gentle swings, and polite applause, but not when Paul Daniels is on the green. He did this thing with the ball where he would putt the ball into the cup, but when the caddy went to retrieve the ball out of the cup, it wasn't there. I have no idea how he did that either but, as he said, "You'll like this….., not a lot, but you'll like this."

Actually, we liked it a lot.

Though I was frequently asked to to continue in an executive role with the BBGV, I have always been a firm believer in the principle that a chairman should not hold the position for more than three years.

I had just left the post when I was approached by someone from a group called Operation Smile, a global organisation based out of the USA. Early on, they had had an office in Hanoi and they ran missions in Vietnam where they went to rural areas and performed a range of operations to repair facial deformities and later cranial deformities. The surgeons, who donated their time, would be flown in, operate for several days on dozens of people, and then fly home. Operation Smile took care of the other expenses and for the pre-care and post-care issues for the patient and the families. They also held training sessions for local doctors and nurses who were make a part of the surgery teams.

I had heard about Operation Smile through a chance meeting with the co-founder of the organisation, William (Bill) Magee in a hotel lobby in 1992 or 1993, but I really didn't know much about them. It was global, but not really that big. I agreed to do the meeting, and the first thing they did was to show me a video of the work that they were doing. I tried to fight back the tears, but without much success. The existing board of directors in Hanoi had fallen apart and they needed a new board in Ho Chi Minh City. After the video was over, I immediately said I wanted to be part of the group. I joined the Vietnam board and in 2001 became its chairman.

My first goal was to pump up the fund-raising so we could refocus the program on coaching and assisting local doctors and nurses to do the surgeries. We would do something like 150 operations per mission and there were two missions per year. This was great, but we all wanted to build up a local network of doctors so that, essentially, there would be no need for missions led by foreign surgeons because it could all be done locally and also year-round.

With Jackie Chan, an Operation Smile Ambassador

We raised money in all kinds of ways, both locally and in the United States and other donor countries with Operation Smile offices, and eventually set up permanent care centres in Hanoi, Hue, and Ho Chi Minh City. These centres were typically set up within existing hospitals and focused on cleft and facial surgeries for children and young adults. Families didn't have to pay anything and the local doctors and nurses also donated their expertise and time. Operation Smile covered the operating costs of the centres and all the expenses associated with the surgeries. During the 10 years that I was heavily involved with the group, we performed something like 18,000 surgeries throughout Vietnam. Imagine that!

Of course, this kind of program requires money and that's where my networking and public speaking skills could be put to good use. The fund-raising pitch was not difficult. I could say something like, "For 250 dollars, you can change a person's life with a simple 20 or 30-minute operation. The Vietnamese doctors do these operations for free, but we still need your help to buy surgical materials." We found a great auctioneer in Hong Kong who was the head of CBRE Asia. He had started life as a cattle

Picture of Ngan and I after her cleft lip and palate surgery

auctioneer and we heard about him from friends in Hong Kong when he auctioned a Mars Bar for US$10,000 in support of the members of the Hong Kong football club who lost their lives in the Bali Bombings. At one event in Vietnam, we arranged for a father and daughter to take the stage and tell their story. The girl was beautiful. She was about seven years old then, but she had been a child with a facial deformity, and had been operated on by our doctors. We had before and after photos displayed as her father told her story. I still have those photos displayed in my office. The father spoke about what it had all meant to his family, but also to all the families in their home village. It changed the girl's life, for sure, but also transformed the family's life and future and really their entire village. Goodness, that was an emotional night. But the result is that you get donors to buy things in an auction that they may never use, for a cause that transcends our ordinary lives, that creates good in the world and a sense of worth for the individual. I still have those photos displayed in my home.

The success with Operation Smile spilled over to other projects such as Newborns Vietnam. This is a UK registered charity that focuses on caring for premature babies and helping to reduce the incidences of premature infant mortality. I was asked to join the Board of Trustees. As with Operation Smile, their whole emphasis was on training and building up the capacity of local doctors and nurses as well as the ability to help families who had babies at home, meaning outside of a hospital environment. This was usually the case in the rural areas. When I first joined the board, I was the only member who was not a medical person. One thing I am proud of was working with the founders and the Ministry of Health to build up and then finance a national curriculum on how to handle and treat premature babies. Because of the changes over the years to the regulations governing foreign

NGOs and how they can raise funds in Vietnam, these successful charities have had to re-invent the way they operate. This was certainly the case for Newborns Vietnam, which remains a great organisation, but it applies to all the other NGOs as well.

I was never in a position to make big donations, but I could make small donations and also donate my time. I was also good at getting people with much deeper pockets than myself to commit to serious amounts of money. I am also very proud to say that my son Michael has similar instincts. On a recent trip down to the Mekong Delta, he came home and said, "Daddy, the people are so poor in the Delta. Do you know how they live?"

"I do," I answered. "You see how lucky you are, right?"

The next day, he started up a collection of toys for kids to send down to the Delta. This makes me very proud. It's a continuation of my belief in networking and pulling people together for a common cause. I have recently learnt that my elder son Jim and his wife, who are currently living in Sri Lanka, are sponsoring the building of a school near where they live. This is to save the children having to travel long distances to the nearest school, as many do not even make the journey because it's too far. This is something else to be proud of.

I also measure my success not just in terms of money, but also by the number of people I have helped to step out of their own comfort zones. One of my favourite stories is about Lizette Crabtree, a young female chef who we were told was one of South Africa's top ten chefs. This would have been in 2001 and 2002. Julie and I were staying in one of our favourite places, Franshoek, which is close to the wine producing region of Stellenbosch in South Africa. We had been recommended to have dinner at a restaurant where she worked. We managed to book a table and we were served one of the most amazing meals I have ever had. I still remember and can even taste the exquisite starter, moules in coconut and sweet chili!

Julie was not too impressed when I asked the waiter if I could meet the chef. She was even less so when a tall blond lady in whites approached the table. After an interesting discussion on her love of fusion cooking, I asked if she would like to come to Vietnam to do a South African food and wine promotion. Julie was aghast and blurted out, "How can you promise something like that?" I said not to worry and, within three weeks of our return to Vietnam, I was able to organise the event with the Asia Reflections restaurant inside the Caravelle Hotel. It was a big hit and six months later Lizette was offered a job as sous chef which she accepted and moved to Ho Chi Minh City. She later became the head of the Sailing Club group in Vietnam where she met her now husband while running the Sailing Club Hotel in Mui Ne. She was also best friends with Julie, who was with her last month in South Africa.

I feel honoured to have lived and worked in Vietnam, and in Ho Chi Minh City in particular, for more than three decades. Of course, it has not always been easy, but it has been a remarkably exciting place to live and work. I am reminded of this on a daily basis, especially when I sit on my perch behind my Nag's Head bar and look at my son, Michael. I wonder if he will lead a life similar to mine, a life of travel and 'small world moments.' I certainly hope so. I'm not sure who will take him on shunting expeditions around railway yards, but as a family we have already taken numerous trips within Vietnam and abroad. I am fortunate to have the financial means to see to his needs in a manner that my parents ultimately provided for me, but not at quite as high a level and at a much higher cost to themselves. It was extremely difficult for them, and a little easier for me catering to the needs of my elder children when they were growing up. Today, it is much easier for Suong and I to care for our son, and this is the consequence of the work ethic and financial prudence, let's call it the Atkinson Traits, that I inherited from my parents.

So in addition to the trips abroad, a private international school education, and all the things that a modicum of financial independence can provide for a child, I hope I can do at least one more thing for my son, which is to pass on to him the Atkinson Traits. From my post at the Nag's Head Bar and with my wine glass raised towards Michael, I commit to doing this just as well for Michael as my parents did for me, and as well as I believe I did for my elder kids.

My two collaborators on this memoir, the British artist Richie Fawcett and the American writer Sam Korsmoe as well as many other people, have asked me a million times about the highest points of my legacy. In a way, I decided to work on this memoir to be able to work out the answer. I have had several 'high points' in my life that I am proud of along with a few lows. My children and grandchildren top the list and I am proud of all

Grant Thornton Vietnam's 30th anniversary in 2024

With Princess Anne around 2001 in Ho Chi Minh City. She later presented me with my OBE

their achievements. On that one, there is no debate. I am proud that Grant Thornton Vietnam celebrated its 30th anniversary in 2024. I am proud that it employs 400 people today. Launching the first British Chamber of Commerce and my work with Operation Smile, Newborns Vietnam, and the Christina Noble Foundation have all been high points of my life and work in Vietnam.

There are two other "accomplishments" that I have only briefly mentioned up to this point, items about which Richie, Sam and others keep asking me to identify which is bigger and more important to me. Is it being granted Vietnamese citizenship and being allowed to have dual nationality by the President of Vietnam? Or being made an Officer of the Order of the British Empire (OBE) by Queen Elizabeth II?

First off, I am beyond grateful and frankly quite surprised that such a question has come to me. There are many OBEs in the world, the exact number is difficult to know. This order was established in 1917. There are records on who has received the OBE, and some estimates put it at around 700 to 800 per year over the past 10 years. Prior to this, it is difficult to really know. Presumably, there were fewer people awarded the OBE in the first few decades of the order, but this is purely conjecture on my part. Again, the fact that I am having to write about this issue and how it relates to my life is astonishing. After all, there are 68 million citizens of Great Britain and in 2022 I was one of about 800 who were awarded an OBE? Astonishing!

I have not yet shared that my father, Albert Atkinson, was awarded an MBE for his services to British exports. To be honest, the idea of replicating my father's accomplishment was in me, but by the time I semi-retired in 2019 and with no such good news, I had stopped thinking about it. I figured I had blotted my copy book, and I even knew when and where I may have done so. For this reason, when I received an invite for lunch in May 2022 with the then acting Consul General Oliver Todd and the Deputy CG and Head of Trade Sam Wood, I wracked my brains thinking what I had done or who I had upset. I had no idea what was about to transpire.

We sat down to lunch in Basilico, a restaurant close to the British Consulate. I have to admit that I had a touch of the collywobbles. Before we really got into the conversation, Oliver announced that they had something important to discuss. He further stated, "There's no easy way to say it other than congratulations. You have been nominated to receive an OBE."

They then explained that they needed my confirmation that I would accept it if confirmed. For one of the few occasions in my life, I was speechless and had a thousand thoughts whizzing around my head.

Oliver broke the silence by asking, "So what do you think?"

I managed to sputter that I felt truly humbled and honoured. I had long ago given up thinking that I would ever receive such an honour, especially at the age of 74. My next thought was my

Mum (who passed in October 2021) and how proud she would have been.

"Of course," I said. "Of course, I would accept."

The OBE was officially gazetted in Queen Elizabeth's last birthday honours on June 2, 2022. I was invited to receive my OBE at Windsor Castle in February 2023. I was hoping to do so in the company of my three children, but Jim had business commitments in the USA and Claire had to have some surgery. My son Michael, Suong, and my cousin Raymond accompanied me to the ceremony.

It was an amazing day starting with lots of coffee and toast and then putting on my morning suit before a 10-minute walk through the streets of Windsor to the castle entrance in Castle Hill at 10 am. The first security check was very relaxed and friendly with the police officer extending his congratulations. We then proceeded to walk up the hill to the Royal Apartments, passing St. George's Chapel, to the second security check. Again, everything was relaxed and jovial and one of the police officers told Michael he was a mini James Bond and presented him with a police badge.

We then entered the Royal Apartments and were directed to the King's ante room with about twenty or so other people who were both recipients and guests. We were asked to wait for a briefing at 10:55. It was only on entering that I received the order of the day and discovered that Princess Anne would be the Royal handing out the honours. I was pleased about this as we had met on two previous occasions in Vietnam.

The proceedings started at 11 am after the briefing. There were a few people with higher honours ahead of us, but as my name starts with an 'A,' I was the first of the OBEs. We were ushered to the Hall with my guests to the left and me to the right watching as the preceding investiture was being carried out. Looking at

Receiving the OBE from Princess Anne

With my family and cousin Raymond

the Grand Hall and Princess Anne in uniform on a low dais with an orchestra playing in the background, I was feeling like royalty if only for a few minutes.

When the investiture in front of me was finished, I was invited

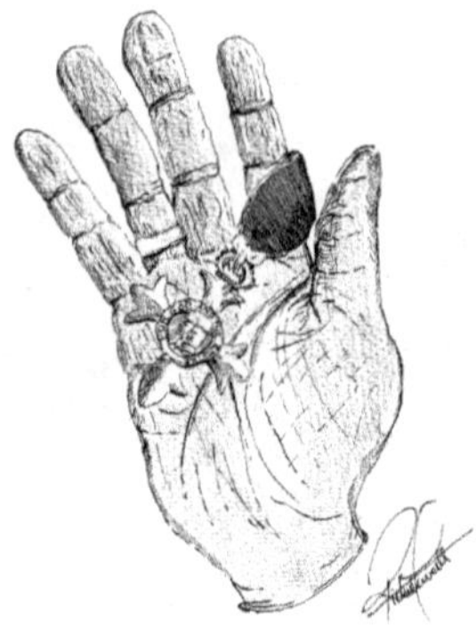

to approach the dais and Princess Anne which I did with a mixture of pride and humility. The conversation with the Princess Royal was relaxed and easy. We spoke about her visits to Vietnam and her last visit when I was then Chairman of BBGV. It was over all too quickly. We then exited the hall with family and the official photographs which took much longer than the audience with her Highness.

After the ceremony and photos, we headed off to a celebratory lunch at one of my favourite old haunts, The Compleat Angler at Marlow, where we were joined by Vietnamese Ambassador Nguyen Hoang Long and his wife. The day will stay with me for the rest of my life and I wear the medal with pride. My only regret is that my Mum was not there to see the day.

As for becoming a Vietnamese citizen, the number of foreigners who have been allowed dual nationality, the *awarding* (I prefer to use that verb instead of 'granted' or 'issued') of Vietnamese citizenship to a non-Vietnamese person is extremely rare. Recently, the Brazilian footballer Rafaelson Bezerra Fernandes, who was born in 1997, was granted Vietnamese citizenship and goes by the name of Nguyen Xuan Son. He is an extremely gifted football player who plays for Vietnam's national football team. There are at least two or three other foreigners who are known to have received citizenship and dual nationality. To my knowledge, that's it. Just three or four others and me.

I first started thinking about the possibility of applying for Vietnamese citizenship in 2015. This was not long after I took the Executive Chairman role at Grant Thornton. I had a number of reasons for doing so, but mainly it was because I knew I wanted to stay in Vietnam. Although I had permanent residency, it had to be renewed every 10 years or whenever I renewed my British passport. Others who I knew had been granted dual nationality did so by virtue of their receiving medals of honour from the Government of Vietnam. I didn't have that, so I decided to do it the hard way and apply through the Ministry of Justice.

It was quite time consuming. I had to demonstrate what I had done to benefit the country and help with its development. Fortunately, I had been an early investor in Vietnam through PCS and subsequently Grant Thornton. I had helped with the training of hundreds of accountants and CPAs. I had received a Certificate of Merit from the Prime Minister of Vietnam for my role in the development of the accounting profession. I was also one of the founders of the first foreign Chamber of Commerce (BritCham). In my role as Chairman of Operation Smile, I had helped change the life of more than 18,000 children with facial deformities. As Chairman of Newborns Vietnam, I was playing a role in reducing infant mortality. This was something close to my heart because my youngest son Michael and I were both born five weeks premature.

I got supporting letters from all the associated organisations. I also let some key people know that I would be submitting an application for dual nationality. One surprise, which I learned about just as I was submitting the final application, was that I needed a Vietnamese name. On the spur of the moment, I assumed my wife's family name of Pham and the names of two good friends, Kien and Son.

About eighteen months later, I was asked to attend a meeting at the Ministry of Justice where I was asked to supply a notarised copy of the Certificate of Merit for which they quoted me full details including the date of issue. In addition, I was asked to sign

With Prime Minister Pham Minh Chinh and other VIPs at the Vietnam Business Forum in 2023

a declaration that if granted dual nationality I would not seek British Consular protection in Vietnam. I signed this declaration.

After that, I just waited. I had really given up hope until in November 2018 when I received a letter from the Ministry of Justice asking me to make an appointment, which I duly did. At that meeting, I was handed the official letter from the President of Vietnam granting Pham Kien Son a.k.a. Kenneth M Atkinson Vietnamese citizenship. There was no ceremony or swearing of allegiance. This was an honour along with a small victory gift as the number of my subsequently issued ID was .....000001!

As far as legacy goes, both the OBE and becoming a naturalised Vietnamese is an honour. There is not one that is higher than the other and neither rises higher than my family. I am confident, though, that I am the only Vietnamese citizen who has ever been awarded the OBE. I am also confident that *in my lifetime* I will remain the only one. After that, I am sure many Vietnamese people will rise to the challenge of earning many international awards, an OBE or others similarly prestigious.

Thank you for joining me on this journey of my life. Working on this memoir at the spritely young age of 76, has been a great joy, and I hope you have also enjoyed my re-telling of a lifetime of tales. From Saddleworth to Saigon, it's been fun to share.

Reflections on Ken Atkinson

Pham Phu Ngoc Trai
Former Chairman of PepsiCo Indochina

A Trusted Companion in Vietnam's Transformation

Vietnam's transformation over the past four decades has been nothing short of extraordinary. From a centrally planned economy to one of the most dynamic and rapidly growing markets in the world, the country has undergone a profound shift – one fuelled by resilience, vision, and ambition. Many have played a role in this journey, but few foreign professionals have had the privilege of not just witnessing but walking alongside Vietnam in its transformation as closely as Ken Atkinson.

I first met Ken in the early 1990s when Vietnam was cautiously opening its doors to the world. At the time, I was leading PepsiCo's expansion into the country, navigating an unfamiliar business landscape filled with challenges and uncertainties. Foreign Direct Investment (FDI) was still in its infancy, regulations were evolving, and trust between international investors and local enterprises was just beginning to take shape. In those crucial years, you needed the right people by your side – people who didn't just offer advice, but truly understood the journey ahead.

That's where Ken stood out. He wasn't just an expatriate consultant passing through. He was someone who saw the potential in Vietnam, believed in its people, and committed himself wholeheartedly to its development. His knowledge of global business was vast, but what set him apart was how he blended that expertise with a deep respect for the culture and ambitions of the Vietnamese business community. He didn't just advise – he partnered, supported, and became a trusted friend to so many including myself.

Over the years, we had opportunities to work together on projects that would help shape Vietnam's business landscape. Together, we worked on various projects related to investment, management,

M&A, business and organisational restructuring, and other strategic initiatives.

During my time leading major corporations like PepsiCo and later with my own company Global Integrated Business Company (GIBC), Ken was always a reliable partner – whether we were discussing talent recruitment, new project development, or navigating strategic challenges.

Ken and I worked seamlessly together because we shared the same values: integrity, trust, and a deep belief in doing what is right. He was never just "doing business" in Vietnam. He was building something greater. He truly cared about the enterprises he worked with, treating them not just as clients but as partners in a shared mission.

If someone were to ask me what I admire most about Ken, I would say his heart. Unlike many who come to new markets looking for business opportunities, Ken built genuine relationships. He didn't just provide a service – he walked alongside Vietnamese businesses through every struggle, every success, every step of their growth.

Beyond his vast professional achievements, Ken is a man of his word. When he makes a promise, he keeps it. In business and in friendship, that reliability is rare, and it is one of the reasons he has earned such deep respect in Vietnam.

Ken's impact goes far beyond finance, investment, or corporate strategy. Long before ESG (Environmental, Social, and Governance) became a global business priority, he was already advocating for responsible growth, sustainable business models, and ethical corporate leadership. He wasn't just talking about the future. He was actively helping to shape it. His influence has left a lasting mark on the Vietnamese business community and will continue to inspire the next generation of leaders.

But more than anything, what I admire most is Ken's deep connection to Vietnam. For many expatriates, a country is just a place to work. For Ken, Vietnam became home. Over the past 35 years, he has built more than businesses. He has built a life, friendships, and a lasting legacy.

Even now, after stepping back from his operational role at Grant Thornton, Ken's passion remains as strong as ever. He continues to mentor, guide, and uplift the business community, always ready to lend his wisdom. His influence is far from over. It is embedded in the very fabric of Vietnam's economic evolution.

This memoir is not just the story of Ken Atkinson. It is the story of a life well lived in service of something greater. Through Ken's eyes, we see the struggles, the triumphs, the sacrifices, and the friendships that have shaped his incredible journey.

Ken's story is a testament to what truly matters: not just financial success, but the relationships we build, the people we uplift, and the impact we leave behind. He has done more than establish businesses – he has earned the love, trust, and respect of an entire nation.

As Vietnam looks to its future, it will be people like Ken, those who believe in its potential, invest in its people, and walk alongside it through every challenge, that will help turn ambition into reality.

To my good friend Ken, thank you for all you have done for Vietnam, and for being the kind of person this world needs more of. I wish you and your beloved family all the happiness in this next chapter, and I know that your impact here will continue to be felt for many years to come.

***

Trung Nguyen Chi
CEO and Managing Partner Grant Thornton Vietnam

Promoter & Partner
The auditing industry in Vietnam is relatively young. I joined it in 1995 as part of one of the first batches of accountants. Ken arrived Vietnam quite early, around 1992 or 1993. In those early days, it was a small industry so everyone more or less knew each other. Though I knew who Ken was, surprisingly I never actually talked with him until around 2010.

The reason for this first meeting was to begin a discussion regarding a potential merger between Nexia ACPA and Grant Thornton Vietnam ("Grant Thornton"). Nexia ACPA ("ACPA"), an auditing and consulting firm that I and other nine partners founded in 2004, was a member firm of Nexia International. At that time, our business was very successful, experiencing strong growth. As a result, we became the 13th largest firm out of more than 100 firms worldwide within six years. However, to prepare for future growth, we decided that we should change to a stronger international network in terms of brand, size, methodology and technical support, and network collaboration. In 2010, ACPA started making plans to share our intentions and to seek a merger with other firms. That's how I ended up meeting with and talking to Ken.

It was a good conversation. I expressed our intention to seek a merger for ACPA and shared our ambitions. We both exchanged information about our respective firms. While we were ready to move forward, it wasn't the right time for Ken. However, we both achieved something valuable: I and our partners got to know Grant Thornton and recognized it as a good firm, and Ken learned the same about ACPA.

Three years later, in 2013, we met again and Ken shared his succession plan. At that time, our two firms were quite similar in size, each with about 110 staff. ACPA was strong in Hanoi, while Grant

Thornton was strong in Ho Chi Minh City. Both firms excelled in audit, but ACPA also had a strong tax practice, and Grant Thornton was strong in advisory services. ACPA had a robust client base among Japanese companies, whereas Grant Thornton had a strong base among Western companies. The cultures of the two firms were quite similar. There was good synergy between our two firms, which led to a swift general agreement to pursue a merger. Ken and I began discussions in the second quarter of 2013, and we successfully completed the merger by July 1, 2014.

The merger brought together a leading professional services firm with an excellent combination of professional team members of 14 partners and more than 220 professional staff in offices located in Hanoi and Ho Chi Minh City. Ken was appointed as Executive Chairman and I was appointed as CEO and Managing Partner. We were all very proud that our merger was one of the most successful mergers both in the auditing industry in Vietnam and within the Grant Thornton International network at that time. In 2024, Grant Thornton Vietnam was ranked the 6th largest auditing firm in Vietnam.

What stands out about Ken?

With over 33 years of working and living in Vietnam, Ken has a deep understanding of the local business environment as well as culture. Ken is a visionary, always demanding high standards on professionalism and quality. He is dedicated to serving clients. I personally learned a lot from Ken since we started working together in 2014. My colleagues and I are always grateful to Ken, the founder, for his great valuable contribution in establishing and growing Grant Thornton into what it is today.

***

Vinh Ha Nguyen
Partner – Head of Advisory Services at Grant Thornton Vietnam

How many bosses would do that?

I can't remember clearly how long I've been here at Grant Thornton, since it's been so long. I graduated from the National University of Economics with an accounting degree in 1996. At that time, I planned to be a professor so I actually started to work at the university, but only for a few months. I quickly realised that it wasn't for me. I left the university and started with Grant Thornton when it was still Bourne Griffiths.

I never left. I know that's a bit unusual because people usually change jobs. I have to say that I thought about leaving the company a few times. I was recruited by headhunters and always with an offer of a higher salary. I even signed an offer agreement from one company and also submitted my letter of resignation. I talked to the partners about it, including Ken even though he wasn't my direct boss at the time, and I changed my mind.

Before I really knew him, I heard Ken had a reputation for being hot-tempered. I would see him now and then, but he wasn't my direct boss, so I couldn't really say that he was like that. However, I have one very clear memory of Ken. I don't remember the year exactly, but it was about 2004 or 2005. The merger between Bourne Griffiths and Grant Thornton had taken place and we were in a new office near the Hong River in Hanoi. It was a very basic office with simple furniture. The building was located on a dike near the river so it was quite exposed to the weather. One day, Ken visited the office. I think for the first time. It was wintertime so we were all wearing full winter clothes because it was so cold. The wind was terrible. You know how Hanoi winters can be. Of course, the building had no heating system.

So when Ken arrived, he saw everyone working away on computers while wearing our winter coats and hats. He toured the office and went to all the floors, up and down several times, going into every room and taking it all in. He then called the office manager in and they went into an office. We were all curious about that. Of course, we didn't know what they were talking about, but a few days later a bunch of heaters started arriving to the office. He organised one for each room so we could work in comfort. It wasn't just for the boss's office, but enough individual heaters for everyone. We were so appreciative because we knew the company was still very small and it wasn't a great time to be making such a large purchase, but he did it anyway. I still get emotional thinking about that. I mean, imagine how many bosses in Vietnam would do that? Not so many.

He cares a lot about people development. We all acknowledge that Grant Thornton has a very encouraging policy to achieve higher qualifications. These are for external training programs inside and outside of Vietnam. Those programs are very expensive. I would say examples include the ACCA courses. Grant Thornton was among the first Vietnamese companies to offer this to the staff. It was also the only one to offer it very widely, almost for all the professional staff. Grant Thornton also sent staff to regional and global training programs of Grant Thornton International. I took part in a New Zealand program which was a great opportunity to learn and gain international exposure.

I was made partner in 2007 and I was the very first Vietnamese promoted to partner at that time. I was quite young. Even if I did have the technical skills and was quite capable, I am sure I was missing things here and there, but Ken was the one. Even though he wasn't my direct boss, he was the one who advocated for my promotion. He did that for everyone, not just me. Ken was a very strong advocator for promotion of local staff to management positions.

He's quite fearless as well. We pitched for a very big project with the Asian Development Bank. We all felt it was too big because we only had around 15 staff and it was a million dollar plus project. Ken mobilised the team and we had people from the Philippines, India, and other experts. It was a very big project and we were competing against a lot of other big consulting companies, but we got it. Wow, fearless. I mean fearless. I wonder if there's a different word that I can use.

Ken is good at networking, of course, but I would say his biggest strength is with people and in being a generalist. He has a very broad knowledge about things. He can make sense of technical ideas even if he's not really a specialist. He can give clients very good advice. He offers that to his staff as well.

I am a partner now for the company's advisory services and have 30 people working directly for me. Grant Thornton was really my first job. I tell the next generation and the people below me to always choose your first employer very carefully. They will end up defining you. They will make you the person that you are going to be. In my case, it is to be professional, honest, open, and direct. Ken has helped me a lot in defining these values.

***

Mark Fraser
Founding Manager Partner, Frasers Law Company Vietnam
Resident of Vietnam from 1995 to present

Pioneer Spirit

I'll have to Google the precise date, but I know exactly where I first met Ken Atkinson. It was at the bar at the Camargue Restaurant, on a Saturday, in June or July 1995, in Saigon. It was the day of the Rugby World Cup Final between New Zealand and South Africa. Now, I'm a New Zealander, and like most New Zealanders, I love sports and rugby in particular which we are all brought up on, playing and watching. The All Blacks is our national team. That was back when Jonah Lomu was playing and they were huge favorites at the World Cup. They had done extremely well all through the tournament. No one was giving South Africa, the Springboks, a chance. So I show up at the bar wanting to make a wager on the match, but no one would take the Springboks. I asked all around and everyone was saying that it's an open and shut case. The All Blacks were going to win.

But, there was one guy sitting at the bar who agreed to take the Springboks. I had to give him exorbitant odds, something like five or ten to one to take the bet. He told me, "Look, I know nothing about rugby. I'm a Manchester United fan, but I'll take the Springboks."

We agreed to a bet of something like $5 or $10 and, of course, we all know what happened. The Springboks won in extra time and I had to pay this guy something like $50. Of course, the guy was Ken. I lost the bet, I'm still sad about the All Blacks losing, but it was the start of a brilliant friendship. That was 30 years ago.

We started working together on the British Chamber of Commerce or, as it was called in the beginning the British Business Group or BBG. We were both board members. From the third year, Ken was the chairman and I was the vice chair. We would encourage and support different activities and initiatives, both social and charity. We basically tried to provide an umbrella group for the expat community led by the Brits or people who worked in British businesses. He was also the deputy chairman of the Vietnam National Authority on Tourism. On the charity side, Ken got involved with Operation Smile in a big way as well as the Christina Noble Foundation.

The character of the man is a very giving guy. He's the kind of guy who you can ring up and say, "Hey Ken, I need to talk to you", and he'll always find time. If he has a slot in his diary, he will make time for you. He works jolly hard.

He is obviously somebody who, early on in his career, decided am I going to be a banker who focuses on residential financing in Manchester? Something like that? No. He wasn't cut out for that. He wasn't that type of person. He has had a pioneer spirit for a long time. When I learned about the Leningrad Hotel project from this project, it was new to me, but not surprising. During the early days of the British Chamber of Commerce, and in particular around 1997 when there was the regional economic crisis, he kept things together for the Chamber. He kept it all moving forward on a shoestring budget. It was funded purely from contributions and membership fees.

When I heard that he was going to try and get Vietnamese citizenship, it didn't surprise me. He has the passion and the commitment to Vietnam. I wasn't surprised that he received it, because if he couldn't get it then no one could. For the OBE, the only surprising thing about that was how long it took for him to get that level of recognition. He deserved it. I tell that to British diplomats and others all the time. When I received the news, I can't believe how happy I was. Oh, I was really, really happy. Such genuine joy. I couldn't think of anyone who deserved it more.

***

Mark Lockwood
Former Baker McKenzie Lawyer
Multi-year resident of Vietnam since the early 1990s

Mixing with The Carpetbaggers

Ken and I met back in 1993 or 1994. I was a lawyer based in Hanoi and Ken was based in Ho Chi Minh City, but we would frequently meet for dinner and drinks when he was in town. Back then, he was considered a finance guy. He had done the Great Wall Hotel in Beijing and a hotel in West Lake. He was speaking at events all the time. He's a very good public speaker. If there was a conference by the Economist or the VIR or whoever, Ken would be up there presenting about Vietnam. But he didn't really have a role or a specialty. Okay, you can be a one-off banker, but he wasn't working for a bank. He was sort of mixing with the carpetbaggers.

He was flying in and out a lot so I told him, "You better get a career here. You better do something." I told him about an accounting firm down the road called Bourne Griffiths. It was run by a competent accountant, but one without any sales skills or ability to grow the business. At the time, Bourne Griffiths was a tiny Australian mid-level accounting firm. They never would have stayed or grown. They were probably here because there were a couple of Australian mining companies floating around in those early days. There were lots of people looking for stuff at the time. They had a couple of clients.

"Maybe you should join them," I told Ken.

"But, I'm not an accountant," he said.

"Well, okay, but it's Vietnam, yeah?" I answered.

He joined up with them and that's how he became an accountant. It gave him a reason to stay here and it gave him credibility. A few years later, he morphed it into Grant Thornton and voila. I think Ken's story is about perseverance. How do you grow something from nothing? From nothing. That's what he did.

He is a great problem solver. If anyone, including us, had a compliance issue, tax issue, or even a legal issue, we would go to Ken and ask, "What's the answer?" He has a great feel for what the answer is. He also works harder than any of his competitors. That's how I think he grew the Grant Thornton business. It has over 400 people today.

The other thing is Operation Smile. I don't want to say it was a two-bit charity, but they were really small. You know, just a couple of doctors coming over to do a couple of operations. Back in the day in Hanoi, there was only one charity that everyone went to and it was Operation Smile because of what Ken did for the organization.

He also worked on the British Business Group, or BritCham. Back then, no one wanted to be chairman, so Ken would always step in. I don't know how many times he's been chairman. It was a case of so-and-so is chairman and then they leave. No one wants to do it. Okay, Ken does it. After a while Ken says, "I don't want to do it anymore." So, someone else turns up and then they leave, and it goes back to Ken again. He's been doing that for 25 years. His community service stands out. He's done more than anyone else. I think he deserved the OBE for that alone.

Today, if I had a serious problem, regulatory, legal, and it is all mixed up, I'd go to Ken and ask, "Ken, what do we do here?" and he would break it down very logically. He's very generous with his time. Not bad for a non-lawyer and a non-accountant.

***

Carl Gay
Founder of Indochine Engineering
Resident of Vietnam from 1997 to 2023

Cradle to Grave

I would have met Ken in the mid-1990s or so. Back then, everyone knew each other in the expat community in Vietnam. The place was smaller than it is now so it was easy to meet people. But our story really begins in 1999 when I set up Indochine Engineering. I needed to establish a company to do engineering work in Vietnam, but I couldn't get it done as a foreigner under Vietnamese law. But what you could do was to set up an offshore company, and use that to setup under Vietnam law, and with Ken's help that's what I did. Back then, a lot of foreigners did the same thing. Using a local company with an offshore parent, we grew in time from a private company to a joint stock company and to an exit.

So, that's how I met and began to work with Ken. What's unique about our relationship is that it continued for so long after getting my offshore company set up. In fact, it continued up until just recently when I sold Indochine Engineering to a Japanese company. Ken was our auditor, advisor, mentor, confidante … and so on for 25 years. I think that's quite unusual. Most people have relationship issues. In some ways, it was like a marriage. Also, I have just the one wife! It seems we were able to tolerate each other for a long time, but Ken's a pretty easy guy to tolerate.

He's got good people skills and he presents well. To a degree, I'm the opposite. I've got good technical skills, different people skills. I guess the word [about Ken] that comes to mind is schmoozer. There are schmoozers with substance and schmoozers without. Ken definitely delivered for us, and in hindsight the nature of Vietnam is that we all learn as we go.

You know, that said, he has taken on some really good roles over time. He led the Brit Cham for years. He was also heavily involved with

Operation Smile. He is also quite tolerant of staff. I go off on them when things went badly, but he would come in and settle everyone down. He's a great networker and he knows a lot of people. I guess that's people skills again which he is really good at.

How would I define our relationship?

It's a cradle-to-grave thing. We started in 1999 and sold in 2024, 25 years later. At the beginning and at the end, Ken was with us the entire time. That's a good thing.

***

John East
Lawyer and friend since the 1970s

Carving His Own Way

I first met Ken when he was with Nordic Bank back in the 1970s. At the time, international banking was moving away from America to primarily London because of something called the USA interest equalisation tax. This drove America's offshore lending to offshore bases rather than staying in America. I was in a firm which was at the forefront of acting for banks outside New York on those kinds of deals. This was back in the 70s. Nordic Bank was involved in a lot of those deals, especially those with a Scandinavian element.

For a lawyer, I was getting a bit of a reputation of putting those deals together. Ken was the same on the banking side. Nordic Bank would be the arranger of the loan that I would draft and then it would be sold to a number of banks. Depending on the size of the loan, it could be 15 to 20 or 30 banks. In those days, there was no internet, of course, so Ken and I had to travel around to negotiate the loan face to face with the various borrowers and the other banks and then we would also travel to get the documents signed after an agreement was reached. At signing, they tended to have quite large celebrations. We traveled to places like Iceland, Scandinavia, North America, Asia, and we even traveled to Moscow for a hotel project that was being built in St. Petersburg/Leningrad for the 1980 Moscow Olympics. In China, they had these huge 14 course banquets and we were feeling pretty ill at the end of some of those. Once, I found Ken with his head stuck in a big Chinese urn or leaning up against it fast asleep. He wasn't in too good of shape and I was probably in a pretty bad way too.

We traveled together a lot and I think we found that we had a sort of mutual liking and respect for each other. We're nearly the same age. We both worked pretty hard. We were both conscientious, but at the same time, we liked to make doing business enjoyable.

I remember the negotiations for the Russia deal. Those loan agreements tended to follow a fairly standard form, but we had to write them all up from scratch. I think now it's all done by AI, but not back then. One of the clauses that was in there was about what happened if a war was declared between the various countries. I tried to raise this issue while in our discussions in Moscow, but I had Ken kicking me under the table trying to make me stop talking about war with Russia [laughing]. We had some entertaining times.

We were really at the forefront of international lending in China when we did the Great Wall Hotel deal in 1978. I remember we flew through Hong Kong and all my luggage failed to arrive, but Ken got me a new suit in 24 hours. We then got on the train into China and then flew up to Beijing. After that, we were just waiting for a meeting because that's how it was back then. I'd come down and say, "Is there a meeting today? No? Not today." So, I'd go off on another sightseeing tour somewhere. But we also had these banquets where the Chinese liked to entertain and Ken and I were pretty tested by them after daylong trips up to the Great Wall or elsewhere when the facilities were still pretty primitive. One problem was that Henry Kissinger had announced on a state visit that he liked Mao Tai (a strong spirit) so that this was automatically the drink provided at all the banquets.

The Great Wall hotel project gave me and my firm, and gave Ken, a bit of a head start for the China market, but China was a tough market for him. Ken was a bit of a small fish for a very large pond so I wasn't too surprised when he upped and went off to pursue his consultancy business in Vietnam. I know things were quite hard at first in Vietnam, but nobody could be more delighted, really, than me that he stuck it out and managed to make a real success of it.

He just had tremendous energy and a really good personality and he was very good at getting deals agreed to and completed. So, you know, those are talents that really make people effective. He really liked to do things which were exciting. He was obviously good at finding ways through his personality and expertise to get people interested in dealing with him rather than any competitor.

How did he influence me?

That's an interesting question, isn't it? I suppose he encouraged my own wanderlust a bit and my desire to try out new things and he certainly helped build up my own CV as an expert in the Scandinavian and the Asian legal banking field. I think that's true. He never tested my ethical side of things, but he made me realise that there are times when you just have to say no to people. For me, he was one of the most fun people to do these deals with, and probably for him, I was one of the most fun lawyers to have on the deals to work with him. However, the fun was only possible as a result of the hard work put in first in getting the various deals successfully completed. I probably had other clients like him who worked for banks, but I never had another client who ended up carving his own way as he did by building a successful consultancy business in a developing country in Asia.

***

Ken Buchanan
Banker, boss and friend since the 1970s

We Were Fearless

After 14 years with the Royal Bank of Canada in London, I was headhunted to set up Nordic Bank, which was created by a group of regional banks from Norway, Sweden, Finland, and Denmark. They wanted a more international presence in what was back then a very fast-moving banking sector in London. I realised that I needed some help. I couldn't do all the work that I wanted to get done, so we employed some headhunters and up pops Ken Atkinson. He was a bit younger than me, but I recognised in him a lot of the things that I had already done. He was very, very business oriented. You wouldn't have put him into the sort of classical banker category. You would have said that he was more of a go-getter. The kind of guy who is looking for business opportunities all the time. He was wonderful at digging them out, sometimes to the point of being almost reckless. I think he frightened the life out of most of my colleagues, but he was really good at digging up business.

I was an institutional man. That was my strength. I was an institutional career banker specialising in credit and Ken wasn't, so in a way we were the perfect team. He would go out and get these deals. I'd look at them, tell him that he was a lunatic, or tell him that he had just found the best thing since sliced bread. It would be my job to put it together and get it approved first by me and then by the board. That was our team approach and Ken was an absolutely wonderful teammate. I would basically set him loose and let him run.

It was an exciting time. We were young and probably over-confident. Nevertheless, we were fearlessly prepared to go where few had been before. One of our Finnish shareholders had established a relationship with a prominent North American businessman who, unusually for that time, had significant contacts in the Eastern Bloc. These contacts resulted in a hotel project in Leningrad which Ken had been made aware of and was following closely. While that was in development, Ken walked into my office one day to tell me that he had been approached by the same people to see if we would be able to put together a financing package for a joint venture to build another hotel – this time in Beijing. My initial reaction was skeptical to say the least, but after discussing the matter further I came to realise that Ken was prepared to give it his all. I told him to see what he could put together. The rest is history. He made it happen.

The Chinese counterpart to this venture was a governmental organisation called China International Travel Service. Nobody had ever heard of them. I mean, China was a different place. It was somewhere over there in the far, far distance. No banks had done any business with the country other than trade finance.

Anyway, Ken goes away and comes back and said that they wanted us to go to Beijing. And so I said, "Okay, we're going, but we better take John with us." This is John East, a lawyer who had been documenting transactions for us in London for some years. He was a young, very talented lawyer. He and Ken had a very good relationship. It was an exciting time, as you can imagine, for two guys who were so young.

We arrived in Beijing and stayed at the old Beijing Hotel, which was a bit grim. For our first meeting with China International Travel Service, we were in this great big hall with sofas arranged all the way around the outside. There must have been 20 or 30 Chinese sitting in there, men and women, all dressed in grey Mao suits. There were three or four seats for us. They made an introductory speech of about an hour and a half, which in the end I had to interrupt in order to start talking about the things that we wanted to talk about. It was freezing cold and all we had on were business suits. Ken chastised me later about interrupting the speech, but we were absolutely freezing. Anyway, it must have been successful, but I have no idea why. To tell you the truth, I will never be sure which person, from the vast array of Chinese people, was the main man.

We had a signed deal, but I knew that we had to syndicate the loan financing and I also knew that it was going to be difficult. At the signing, I had to give a speech so I started telling them that we were going on a journey together. The journey was going to be long and there would be ups and there would be downs, but we had to stick together and show the world it could be done. I didn't realise the impact of that speech. I was subsequently told that a lot of the Chinese were relating my speech to Mao Zedong's famous speech about the Long March. I'd never heard of the Long March. It was purely coincidental, but it seemed to seem to do the trick.

How did Ken influence me?

Oh, enormously. Enormously. I had run myself ragged all over Scandinavia, all over North America, all over the place putting deals together and building the bank's portfolio up to the point where somebody else had to pick it up and run with it. If Ken hadn't come along, I don't know what I would have done. He picked up the ball and ran with it. He helped me build my career by doing my stuff. I saw in him all the things that I saw in myself 10 years before. He had the same driving ambition. He had the technical ability. He was bright and intelligent, and he was really determined to succeed.

***

Current Appointments

British Chamber of Commerce – Board Member

Deep C – Adviser

Dynam Capital – Alternate Director

Grant Thornton – Senior Adviser

Nam Long Investment Corporation – Independent Director & Audit Committee Chair

Hai Vuong Sanctuary – Independent Director & Audit Committee chair

Thien Minh Group – Nominee Director for IFC

Vietnam Tourism Advisory Board – Vice Chairman

Dedication

Family photo July 24, 2024 in Wells, UK

I want to remember my mother Mary who was always there for me. She was the first person I would share good news with along with my father Albert. She was a huge supporter and also my fiercest critic. I treasure the five years we had together when she moved to Saigon even though she was never the easiest person to get along with. She taught me a lot of the ethics that have helped me on my journey.

I want to say thank you to each of my wives and partners, who at different parts of my journey were there for me. I am sorry that things did not always turn out as planned.

Linda for bearing two great kids, James and Claire, and sharing my first years as a banker and home builder.

Kathy for helping me launch my own business and working with and supporting me for a few years.

Julie for being there for me during my cancer surgery and beyond and also for standing by me as I was building the business here in Vietnam. I also want to thank her for introducing me to the wonders of my now favorite overseas country, South Africa.

Suong who has helped me integrate more into the Vietnamese community and family life. Thank you for delivering and so lovingly caring for our son Michael. Our son is my new opportunity at parenting, as well as an opportunity to bring up a child in a different age, with the knowledge and time that I did not have with my elder two children.

To Jim and Claire for the times we shared together along the journey and for the close relationship we still enjoy.

I am beyond grateful to all of you. Thank you.

ACKNOWLEDGEMENTS

So, why a memoir? In July 2023, I celebrated my 75th birthday. This milestone and an article written for C Vietnam[1] by Selene Alcock (a writer based in Saigon) entitled **Never Say No** prompted me to think about documenting my experiences for my children, grandchildren, friends, and colleagues around the world. This book's title is adopted from that article. While this memoir serves as a legacy for my family, it also offers insights, humour and entertainment aimed at a broader audience.

Writing a memoir inevitably involves some self-promotion, but I've undertaken projects that I believe are worth sharing. For instance, in 1979/80, I arranged financing for a large hotel project in Leningrad (now St. Petersburg) in the Soviet Union and the Great Wall Hotel in Beijing in China. These early career milestones were followed by many other significant achievements, culminating with being awarded the Officer of the Order of the British Empire (OBE) by Queen Elizabeth II and obtaining Vietnamese citizenship and dual nationality with the formal approval of the President of Vietnam.

I want to share these stories primarily to highlight the value of networking. Instead of chatting over drinks at The Nag's Head or my favourite Saigon watering holes, I'm here aiming at larger audience. I've also included reflections from friends, clients, and colleagues to provide additional perspectives.

This book is structured into chapters that reflect specific time

1 C Vietnam is the official Publication of the Business Executive Network

periods and countries, filled with anecdotes, sketches, photos, and traveler's tales. I hope you enjoy the illustrations by the Saigon-based British artist Ritchie Fawcett and the narrative shaped by Saigon-based American writer Sam Korsmoe.

This memoir chronicles my personal journey, but also touches on broader themes such as globalisation, expatriate life, retirement, and the impact one can make on an adopted country. It's a story of stepping out of one's comfort zone, embracing new cultures, helping others, and constantly networking to achieve success.

From Saddleworth to Saigon, from banking to consulting and auditing, and now to semi-retirement, I have been fortunate to have had such a fascinating journey and I am grateful to everyone who has helped me along the way.

In particular, I would like to thank:

The Partners of Grant Thornton and in particular
Nguyen Chi Trung for sponsoring and checking
the Vietnamese translation of this memoir;

The clients and friends who have generously
contributed their time and memories in their
reflections of me. There has been nothing written that
I do not agree with;

And thank you to Richie Fawcett, who started me on
the journey of producing this memoir
and for his original sketches, and to Sam Korsmoe,
who assisted in its writing. Without you two, this
memoir may never have happened.

my thanks and appreciation to one of Vietnam's
favourite photographers Louis Sang for his time and
efforts to get a cover picture for the Memoir

I would also like to thank you, the reader. I hope you have enjoyed these stories and thank you for picking up this book.

Ken Atkinson
Nag's Head Bar
Saigon, Vietnam
April 2025

About The Author

Ken Atkinson OBE, AKA Pham Kien Son, born and raised on the edge of the Saddleworth moors in northern England, overcame the hardships of post-World War II life with a mixture of smarts, grit, and a solid work ethic instilled by his parents. Ken's pioneering spirit took him to Leningrad and Beijing where he negotiated and financed both country's first ever foreign financed luxury hotels in 1979 and 1980. He eventually arrived in Vietnam where he built a 400-member international accounting firm that recently celebrated its 30th anniversary.

www.ingramcontent.com/pod-product-compliance
Lightning Source LLC
LaVergne TN
LVHW022209200926
848481LV00006B/1911
* 9 7 8 9 8 8 8 9 0 4 4 1 9 *